I0048643

PRAISE FOR *CHANGE TO WIN*

"*Change to Win* is a comprehensive overview of all the tools and management skills required in today's rapidly changing environment. Continuous improvement and the never-ending search for better business models are the prerequisites for both success and survival. This book, based on Rias Attar's practical business experience in both turnarounds and growth situations, is a toolkit on which successful execution can be based. It is a must-read for managers and business owners embarking on transformational projects."

KEN ALLEN, Global CEO, DHL eCommerce Solutions, and author of *Radical Simplicity*

"*Change to Win* captures the critical importance of understanding changing business environments and how innovative corporate leaders can cogently and effectively deliver a winning business model by the integration of strategy, workforce capabilities, culture, and project management! It is a must-read for all business leaders and business students!"

JAN JONES BLACKHURST, Board Member, Caesars Entertainment, and Former Mayor of Las Vegas

"With the patience and skill of a natural teacher, Rias Attar explains the fundamentals of business strategy and implementation and illustrates what it really takes to orchestrate change successfully. Rich with useful frameworks and real-world examples, *Change to Win* is a go-to toolkit for continual adaptation—what every business leader must master in today's age of change."

JOE JACKMAN, CEO, Jackman Reinvents, and author of *The Reinventionist Mindset*

CHANGE TO WIN

How to Optimize or Transform Your Business to Deliver Positive Results

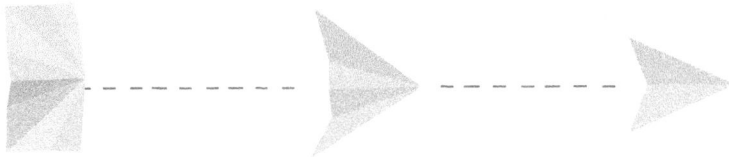

RIAS (GIATH) ATTAR

MBA, PMP, CMP, ACP, CSM, LSSBB

sayAplus Books

Copyright © 2020 by Rias (Giath) Attar

All rights reserved. No part of this book may be reproduced, stored in a retrieval system or transmitted, in any form or by any means, without the prior written consent of the publisher, except in the case of brief quotations, embodied in reviews and articles.

ISBN 978-1-7353339-0-8 (paperback)
ISBN 978-1-7353339-1-5 (ebook)

Published by ⟁ sayAplus Books
www.sayaplus.com

Produced by Page Two
www.pagetwo.com

Edited by Amanda Lewis
Copyedited by Steph VanderMeulen
Proofread by Alison Strobel
Cover and interior design by Jennifer Lum
Interior illustrations by Michelle Clement

www.sayaplus.com

To my hero, my mother, Amira

To my beloved late father, Nazeeh, and to my siblings,
Imad, Lina, and my other hero Suha

To my beautiful loving wife, Sarab, and to our wonderful
and amazing kids, Sarah, Amir, and Yousef

Thank you for all of your love and support
that made me who I am.

I love you all

Contents

PART THREE
CULTURE, CAPABILITIES, AND CHANGE MANAGEMENT

PART FOUR
READINESS FOR UNEXPECTED EVENTS

INTRODUCTION

Change to Win

Over the past few years, we have seen exponential change across industries, faster and more frequently than ever before. It is now the norm for organizations to deal with continual shifting due to factors such as technology, politics, pandemics, and globalization. Unfortunately, many companies have not been able to catch up quickly enough to frequent and wide-ranging changes in the marketplace. Many of them are stuck in the "we have always done it this way" mentality. That standpoint has become their own death sentence. However, it may not be too late for those companies to avoid that business death sentence and effectively change to win.

Consider the famed Fortune 500 companies, the largest US corporations by total revenue for their respective fiscal years. Of the Fortune 500 companies identified in 1955, when the list began, only about 10 percent still exist. To be precise, as of 2019, the number of those companies that still make the list is 52 out of 500.[1] At the current churn rate of disruption, about half of the remaining Fortune 500 firms will be wiped out in the next ten years.

Who could have imagined that nearly nine of every ten Fortune 500 companies would have gone bankrupt, merged, or fallen off the list?

If this is the case for the powerful Fortune 500 companies, how could smaller organizations have survived disruption over the past decades? While we do not have credible data on the exact percentage of smaller companies that have lost their glow over the past sixty years or so, we can safely assume that many of them share a similar fate.

After all, dinosaurs were also big, strong, and powerful. But when the environment changed, they could not adapt and therefore were among the first to go extinct. As Leon C. Megginson said, "According to Darwin's *Origin of Species*, it is not the most intellectual of the species that survives; it is not the strongest that survives; but the species that survives is the one that is able best to adapt and adjust to the changing environment in which it finds itself."[2]

We can anticipate more big changes and disruption in the next decades. Today, companies and their shareholders have high expectations and demand higher profit. Customers continuously demand better quality, lower prices, and better service. But how can a company change to win when the dividing forces of shareholders and customers pull in different directions?

While many organizations feel that change is a threat, others that generally succeed operate under the belief that change brings opportunities to improve products, services, technologies, people, and processes to realize a sustainable competitive advantage. In recent years, many businesses have focused on transforming and optimizing their operations to meet evolving market demands or to keep up with changes in their environments. However, many efforts fail because one or more of the following three pillars do not get leadership's proper attention: Strategies and Tactics; Delivery and Project Management; and Culture, Capabilities, and Change Management.

Companies invest a great deal of money to transform their business. Then they hire consultants to help them draw new objectives. The consultants usually come in, work with the leaders, and document a new strategy using neat presentation slides backed by extensive research. Then, a fat budget is approved and funded, the C-suite announce the strategy in town halls, on bulletin boards, in and emails. Employees are told that they have to change, initiatives are all identified, then then... nothing happens! The companies hit major roadblocks, sometimes as soon as they start transforming their businesses.

Here are some examples of why business transformations fail:

Strategies and Tactics

- Poor leadership
- Unclear strategy, open to interpretation
- Incorrect assumptions
- Lack of innovative or quality-oriented mindset
- Strategy excludes different functions or operations
- Strategy relies on adopting unproven technology
- Lack of customer-centric approach

Delivery and Project Management

- Unrealistic expectations
- Underestimation of effort
- Inadequate resources or budget
- Poor project management discipline
- Lack of action and follow-up
- Poor attention to details
- Not seeing the whole picture or losing focus on the true target
- Overburdened resources with too many initiatives

Culture, Capabilities, and Change Management

- Suboptimal culture
- Poor communication
- Misalignment between key stakeholders
- Management behavior does not support change
- Employees are resistant to change
- Lack of involvement or adoption
- Poor attention to the needs of evolving capabilities

It is a three-legged stool: in order for organizations to be stable and deliver their objectives, all of the elements in each category must be addressed with adequate balance.

Companies and individuals often avoid addressing disruption because it is messy and uncomfortable. But the worst thing business leaders and executives can do is convince their crew that the problem will take care of itself. Sweeping dirt under the rug is a recipe for disaster. Organizations need to combine vision and energy to ensure they are always taking care of their customers and immediately addressing issues or needs. Change is not easy, but not changing can be fatal. Hiding from disruption while not preparing for changes in the marketplace not only causes organizations to stay in their closed-box mentality but also could lead to irreversible business loss. Leaders should always be strategically preparing for and embracing disruption, so they can turn a potential problem into an opportunity.

This book also dives into the most common reasons for failure in business. I show you that often, businesses face a doom-and-gloom fate as a result of leaders and business owners who continue to use the same methods because of past success, and who are uncomfortable taking educated risks and changing approaches and habits. I show you not only why the disruption is happening but also what organizations need to do, when they should act, how they should operate, where they should dig in, who should take the lead, and how much they need to invest in growing and sustaining a competitive advantage.

Changing to win should be the focus in the transformation scope of work. Changing for the sake of change without a clear winning strategy is a waste of time and resources, and it is meaningless without a defined brighter future. Winning can take different forms such as winning market share, increasing the company's value, expanding footprint, boosting sales volume, and improving profitability or cash flow. The winning strategy should define an organization's values, how customers will realize and appreciate those values, what competitive advantages will be created, what differentiation in the market would look like, and how continuous improvement will be structured to ensure the sustainability of the values and competitive advantages created.

It is possible to keep shareholders, customers, employees, and communities satisfied in comprehensive and meaningful ways. By adopting an action-oriented mindset and customer-centric approach, and leveraging proven technology, you will be able to embrace change, build a healthy workplace culture, and deliver positive results within and outside of the company.

Why is it not working anymore? We have always done it that way!

Why does our revenue continue to decline?

Why is our profitability decreasing over time?

Why is our market share shrinking?

Why are our products and services not appealing to our customers anymore?

Why is it becoming increasingly difficult to sustain margin?

PART ONE

STRATEGIES AND TACTICS

1

Why Is Our Model Not Working?

Many businesses and their shareholders are asking why organizations are unable to continuously meet or exceed expectations, keep customers happy, and increase profits. Really, it is the fault of the changing market conditions, technology, and businesses' unwillingness to respond to those changes fast enough.

Market disruption is being driven by the endless pursuit of sales and profits that normally come from serving customers with competitive prices, quality products or services, innovative features, and from offering great customer service. Customers nowadays are seeking products and services with more options and functions, lower prices, higher quality, and faster delivery. This is fueled by competitors trying to lure those customers with more tempting offers and incentives. How can a business compete in this space?

Before jumping into "what to do about it?" it is important to identify and analyze the forces that are continually disrupting the business models and shifting directions:

- Market conditions
- Customer demands
- Technologies

- Competition
- Input costs
- Mergers and acquisitions (M&As)
- Crises and catastrophic events

While these may not be the only factors impacting organizations, all forces can be categorized in one of these seven areas. In the spirit of embracing change, I will give examples of positive sides to every condition that may negatively impact business.

FORCES DISRUPTING BUSINESSES

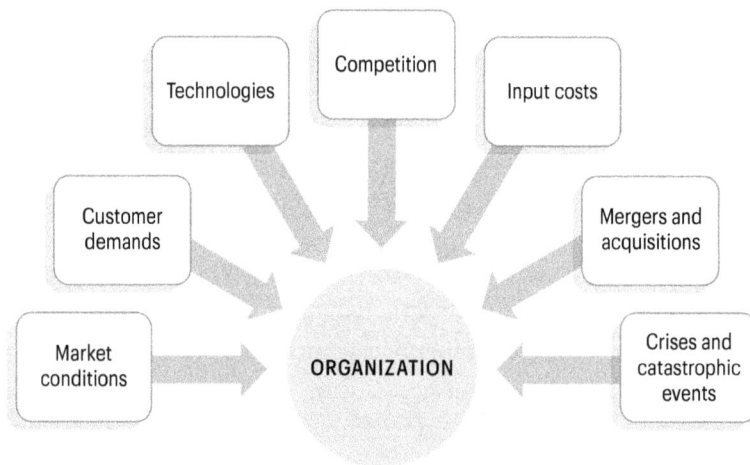

Market conditions: Market-related conditions can generally be divided into three "not mutually exclusive" subcategories: natural, government, and economy-related.

- Natural factors: Climate change and natural disasters can have a severe impact on businesses. While natural disasters can be unpredictable and have sudden and severe catastrophic impact, climate change is slower and has a long-term impact on costs and the business environment. For example, a hurricane or earthquake can be cata-strophic to local businesses, destroying infrastructure. However, they may also create opportunities for other businesses. Construction jobs and flipping houses flourished after Hurricane Harvey in Texas and Hurricane Katrina in Louisiana. Climate change can reduce the availability of raw materials and disrupt the supply chain. It can also force businesses to relocate to avoid water shortage or raising water levels. However, this factor may create opportunities for other businesses to flourish, such as new transportation channels near the North Pole, which could result in reduced cost and shorter mileage.

- Government factors: Any changes in government policy direction or elected personnel in local, federal, or foreign governments can have a big impact on the businesses operating in those areas. These can include monetary and fiscal policies, security, regulatory mandates, permits, immigration policies, and tariffs or trade allowances. For-eign policies may ease or limit certain access to different markets to buy raw materials or sell finished or partially finished goods. While some of those may affect import or the ability to export, they may also create opportunities to find alternative local distribution channels or raw materials. A security threat or mandate may cause citizens anx-iety but could boost surveillance and security companies' business.

- Economy-related factors: Of course, the general economy is another major factor that impacts any business. Some examples include monetary policy, exchange rates, unemployment, inflation, demo-graphic changes, consumer confidence, and energy cost. Again, with any change that could negatively impact the current state of any business, there could be a chance for that same business and/or other business to benefit if they think outside of the box. For example, with an increase in minimum wage, businesses may look for technology that can be substituted for humans; with changes in demographics, businesses may realize the potential of a whole new market that never existed before.

Customer demands: Customers nowadays are mobile-enabled and information-rich. They have unprecedented power, the power of data and access. They have access to information at their fingertips. Within seconds, they can compare offerings and prices, read reviews, ask questions, get answers, and post ratings. The increased popularity, functionality, and speed of mobile devices, including smartphones and smart watches, have given customers the power to disrupt businesses. They are demanding services, products, and experiences that are safer, better, faster, easier, more convenient, and cheaper. Savvy, better-informed, and less loyal customers will switch and go anywhere for what they want. Retaining old customers, attracting new ones, and predicting what they want and when they want it is an art and a science that companies have to master to survive in the current business environment.

Keep in mind that the most common and impactful disruption is driven by customers. They are the driving force in changing demand pattern, adopting new technologies, and changing usage. Customers are choosing Airbnb over big hotel chains, Amazon over big retail outlets, Netflix over cable, and Uber over taxis and car rental companies. But again, customers are asking for safer, better, faster, and cheaper alternatives to fulfill their needs. New, smaller companies are able to change and adapt easier than the big "Titanics," which typically cannot change course fast enough to avoid an iceberg. So, when it comes to meeting or exceeding customers' expectations, new companies benefit from the disruption that is caused by consumers to generate new experiences and offerings that fulfill their needs.

Technologies: The accelerated advancement of technology and the Internet is driving disruption in today's business environment. Investing in or acquiring new technologies should be the top priority of companies in general. Start-ups do not have technical debt to worry about or migrate from. They are able build their infrastructure based on the latest technologies, and move fast to accommodate customer demand, adopt innovation, and take risks because they do not have the burden of connecting, integrating, or even migrating from legacy systems. Older companies are currently trying to embrace digital transformation and move to the cloud; however, that journey takes years, and it is full of challenges and issues, mainly due to data integration and system compatibility.

Technology advancement is happening so fast that companies are finding it hard to catch up and adapt to the latest and greatest capabilities. Robots and artificial intelligence (AI) are replacing people in the workforce. 3D printing allows anyone to create physical items from digital blueprints. Machine learning (ML) analyzes loads of data, identifies patterns, and makes split-second decisions that an average human could take nearly a lifetime to process. Information technology innovation creates new opportunities every day to make more money, be more efficient, find new markets, and change existing operations dynamics.

Competition: Whether a company is a market leader or a follower, competitors always try to grab a part of their market share by introducing new features and offerings or by lowering their cost and prices. In the current global market, competition can come from anywhere. Pressure does not only come from existing competition; it can also penetrate from other competitors trying to find a new niche. For example, McDonald's was mainly a burger chain, but when it entered the coffee and breakfast business, it presented serious trouble for restaurants operating in that segment. New, small competitors can gain market share through innovative offering—for example, consider Uber and how it presented a new solution that utilized advanced technology with minimal capital to invade the taxi business. M&As may present a threat to companies in their market, as synergies realized from those M&As may put pressure on other companies operating in the same marketplace.

It is very important to watch out for competition and defend the business turf. However, it would benefit companies to keep an open mind and think of competition as a unique opportunity to improve their business. Many companies are often their own biggest competitors—refusing to change, ignoring leading indicators, being egocentric about their size and strength, thinking myopically and not strategically, and believing that they will continue to flourish because they have always succeeded doing things a certain way. Today's competition should be viewed as a force that pushes you forward, expands your vision, and allows you to create new opportunities and reach new heights with unique concepts, exploiting areas that have never been touched.

While many services and products can be replicated easily, competition cannot easily copy culture and strong human assets. There is nothing more powerful than employees willing to go above and beyond to serve their organizations. That, of course, is not the only factor that positions any business for success. This strong culture should be part of a solid strategy and well-executed dynamics.

Input costs: The cost of materials, energy, and labor increases every year by an average of 4 percent. Companies always seek opportunities to lower those costs to increase profitability or be more competitive in the marketplace.

Organizations have been trying to find ways to do more work with fewer employees, and produce more outputs with less energy and fewer materials. Most of the time, any dollar saved in those cost categories is a dollar added to the bottom line. Most top executives would agree that increasing labor costs are their biggest concern. Hiring quality employees who reduce rework, increase productivity, and satisfy customers is also becoming challenging. Many of those employees are attracted to certain growing industries, companies, or cities, and it is becoming harder every day to keep them satisfied. The cost of attracting, hiring, keeping, and replacing talent is high. The continued increase to minimum wages, insurance costs, and medical and other benefits add a lot of burden on companies' profit and loss (P&L) statements. Stricter immigration policies limit the ability to bring cheaper labor from other countries. Changes to trade agreements may limit the ability to outsource labor to cheaper countries or import cheaper materials in order to reduce production cost and be more competitive in the marketplace.

Energy and material prices increase as well, and it is getting harder to find efficient alternatives. Rent and real estate prices are also increasing, and companies have no option to sustain margin other than transferring all of these costs to the customers. There are many creative ideas that companies can adapt to reduce overhead costs. Using self-serve options such as kiosks, e-commerce, and mobile capabilities eliminates the need for real people doing the work for customers. Utilizing best-in-class technology would make the process even more appealing to the newer generations of customers who are becoming more technology-savvy than the previous generations. Some companies are encouraging employees to work from home to save on costly office rent. Other companies are utilizing renewable energy to power their facilities while finding alternative raw materials and solution providers that could offer significant savings that help improve the bottom line.

Mergers and acquisitions (M&As): Companies try to merge or acquire each other in an effort to enter new markets, grow market share, realize synergies, and become more profitable as a combined entity. In the past twenty-plus years, M&A has been popular in the business world, but the journey is not always rosy, as many of those deals end up falling apart or not realizing the benefits that were outlined in the business case. But even when well-executed, M&A deals cause disruption to both companies' internal and external processes, cultures, technology platforms, and data flow. M&A deals usually cause significant changes in leadership, positions, priorities, roles, responsibilities, and required skills.

Also, blending two cultures, fully synchronizing and getting people and customers from both companies to fully align and buy into the new culture, can be a challenging months- or yearlong mission. Processes may be similar at both companies, especially if they operate in similar environments, but chances are that there are still big differences and disconnects. Complete process redesigns may be required to allow operations in both companies to work smoothly together. That might require technical work but also huge change management efforts to allow people to adapt to the new processes. Merging technologies and data flow may be one of the biggest hurdles during M&A, as different companies may have different software, hardware, and data architecture. Aligning and combining those elements is not an easy undertaking, and it can be quite costly and lengthy depending on the size of both companies and the disparity of technology levels they may have.

Some examples of the most successful M&As during the past few years include Disney buying Pixar in 2006 and Marvel in 2009, Google buying Android in 2005, Exxon buying Mobil in 1998, Facebook buying Instagram in 2012, Heinz and Kraft merging in 2015, and Dow Chemical and DuPont merging in 2015.

Some examples of M&A disasters in the past years include Quaker Oats and Snapple in 1994, America Online and Time Warner merging in 2000, Sprint's acquisition of Nextel in 2005, New York Central and Pennsylvania Railroads merging in 1968, Daimler-Benz and Chrysler merging in 1998, and Sears and Kmart merging in 2005.

Crises and catastrophic events: By definition, a crisis is a condition of significant instability that could pivotally change all future events, usually for the worse. Some may think of natural disasters such as tsunamis and earthquakes, or of epidemics. Crises may also occur as a result of sudden danger caused by people or the market, such as the September 11 terrorist attacks, the 2008 sudden market meltdown, or the 2020 COVID-19 virus that halted the world for months. Generally, people remember these types of events by referring to the before and after, or where they were when the events happened. For example, people say things like, "Before 9/11, we were able to meet our loved ones at the arrival gates; after 9/11 everything changed forever, and we were not able to do so anymore." Or, "I was walking my dog when John F. Kennedy was shot. After that, all presidential security measures changed forever."

A business crisis is a catastrophic event that can threaten the success or even the existence of that business. Usually the damage to the business operations, at least in the short term, is massive and impacts the financial trajectory, customers, shareholders, communities, and employees. While many crises are external, such as natural disasters, others can be internal, such as the unethical behavior of one of the senior leaders, one faulty product that causes harm to customers, or the mishandling by an employee that results in a big lawsuit.

Take, for example, the Enron disaster, when a few senior executives cooked the books and were so driven by greed that eventually they were all sent to jail while the company and its auditing firm collapsed forever. All financial professionals now know that the Sarbanes–Oxley Act of 2002 was formed to prevent such behavior through stringent audit mandates. There are many examples in the food industry of listeria or salmonella outbreaks that caused illness or death in certain cases, which in turn caused companies' reputation to become tarnished no matter how hard they tried to change all their processes, training, and handling to avoid future issues.

While some catastrophic events, such as COVID-19, are unpredictable, many businesses can have a contingency plan in place in case of a crisis. Organizations should be ready to act fast through a "crisis management plan" that addresses each stage of a potential crisis, from warning to risk assessment, then response, management, resolution, and recovery. This topic will be covered in detail in Part Four of this book.

2

Why Are We Here in the First Place?

I t is easy to draw a dark picture and be negative about new challenges in the business environment. The point is that most successful people work hard to reach certain heights and achieve a certain status. But once they are there, they often become complacent and relaxed, and fall into a trap that causes the deterioration of that brilliant status, and thus the death of their business.

We can always point fingers and blame factors around us, such as the economy, competition, globalization, and political pressure. But what matters most is what actions we take; how we can think and act differently; and if we are capable of adapting to change and finding a chance in the new environment, and willing to do the work.

Nothing happens in isolation; a breakthrough or new technology that impacts production or service may affect current revenue streams and create new customer demands or alternative offerings, but it may also spark new opportunities. Too many companies keep reminding themselves about the glory they once had but never see new areas to explore that could get them to reach new heights, more significant than the legacy they once established.

TRUE OBJECTIVES

Before starting to explore changing our approach, it is important to pause for a moment, take a step back, look at the broader picture, and realign on the purpose of businesses. No matter what the industry is, business objectives should be structured around addressing the following four pillars.

Shareholder satisfaction: Unless the business is a charity or non-profit, it should function first and foremost to serve the shareholders and maximize profits. Increasing cash flow, boosting an organization's value, and/or distributing higher earnings per share will always be the primary target of any for-profit business.

Keeping shareholders happy and up to date is an ingredient for the continuity of a business. When shareholders are satisfied and informed, they typically support business leaders when the time comes to make decisions to redefine a strategy or tactic that could potentially add more value. Maybe one decision is to reinvest surplus cash flow instead of distributing earnings to shareholders; another, to explore investing in a merger, acquisition, or even divesture. Ultimately, any decision should make the shareholders satisfied with increased profits and/or value of their investment.

Even if the organization is a charity or nonprofit, the objective is to satisfy the incumbents or constituents and to deliver certain obligations to meet the objectives outlined in their mission statement.

Customer satisfaction: Meeting or exceeding customer satisfaction translates to how happy they are with a product, service, or experience. Many companies launch surveys to measure customer satisfaction, and they analyze customers' feedback to find where they did well or missed the mark. Organizations also rely heavily on social media these days to check customer ratings, using Yelp, Facebook, Google, Tripadvisor, Expedia, and many other platforms. Customers usually reflect on how they feel about a certain offering from an organization. If they are unhappy, they stop buying the company's products and services, which could eventually bankrupt that company. It is in a business' best interest to increase its customer base, keep customers active, maintain and improve customer satisfaction scores, improve end-to-end customer experience, and continually evaluate the customer journey. The customer journey starts before a transaction or purchase and ends long after it is complete. I will address the journey in chapter 5.

Employee satisfaction: Quality employees are a company's biggest asset. Good employees take care of customers and find ways to save the company money and bring in more revenue. There are many theories on employee satisfaction, but in general, employees should have a combination of the following elements: motivation, empowerment, proper treatment, a sense of achievement, protection and security, and fair compensation.

It is important to note that employee satisfaction can be different from employee engagement. Employee satisfaction can lead to retention and positive culture. Employee engagement usually incites passion and encourages workers to go the extra mile to serve the company and its customers.

Generally, employee satisfaction can be elicited by providing flexible work hours, a good work environment, and better pay and benefits than the competition. Engagement can be boosted only by positive and inspiring leadership. A company can have low-performing but satisfied employees—for example, a complacent employee who is doing just enough work to stay employed while being fully satisfied with the predictable pay and stable employment.

Leaders should focus on having employees with an entrepreneurial mindset, which is key to succeeding in today's environment (more on this in Part Three).

Community satisfaction: Organizations do not exist in a vacuum. The power of the community in supporting businesses is increasing, thanks again to social media and easily accessed and shared information. "Community" means the environment in which an organization exists. It includes the local residential and commercial bodies, suppliers, and vendors; it also includes the social communities that exist in cyberspace.

Helping local communities with donations and sponsorships, and supporting schools, law enforcement, hospitals, and the environment provides tremendous goodwill publicity for organizations. Local municipalities and governments also appreciate those companies that are active in helping their causes and making their communities stronger and safer. In turn, communities would come to aid companies that continually support them. Upsetting a community or having no community presence does not help an organization's efforts to succeed in the marketplace.

Positive word of mouth, online publicity, media and social media engagement, and domestic support are only a few elements that can help a company succeed. In recent years, the cyber community has gained strength and effectiveness in promoting businesses. How many followers and reviews a company has on social media, what suppliers and vendors are posting, what information partners are sharing, what influencers and sponsors are posting—all of these can be great tools organizations can utilize to increase engagement in new markets or grow in existing markets. Those efforts can also help in finding more partners, investors, and quality employees. The better a company's reputation, the better the chances to do more business, find new ways to be more efficient, and discover new partnership opportunities.

The secret of increasing profits and sustaining competitive advantage is continuously delivering value to customers, investing in employees, innovating with and utilizing technology, and supporting local and cyber communities. Meeting or exceeding the expectations of those four stakeholder groups is vital to the success of any organization. Maintaining perfect balance in the satisfaction of shareholders, customers, employees, and the community should be your area of focus. Distributing all profits to shareholders would not enable a company to reinvest in its capabilities and find new horizons. Focusing only on satisfying customers or employees would erode the company's margins and lower or even erase profits. Focusing only on the community would turn a company into a nonprofit organization. Alternatively, neglecting shareholders would mean that executives would not have much support from the owners of the company, and that could put their jobs at risk. Losing focus on customers simply means customer and business loss. Not addressing employees' needs would cause low morale and lack of fulfillment of the company's needs. Not satisfying the community would lead to a loss of their support and could tarnish the company's reputation in the community.

SAFETY FIRST

Before working to satisfy the needs of shareholders, customers, employees, and the community, it is vital that organizations ensure the protection of these stakeholders at all times.

- Protecting the shareholders' interests and the businesses they are investing in is a priority. Never jeopardize safety for better, faster, and cheaper offerings. It is the job of the top leaders in a company to cascade that mandate to all of their employees and embed it in the workplace culture. There is no point in satisfying shareholders if that puts the company in imminent danger. Safety involves not only people but also regulations, ethics, and security (physical and cyber). Shareholders' happiness will likely not live long if leaders or employees bend rules and expose the company to bigger problems. Think about compliance—if employees try to meet or exceed targets without meeting compliance mandates, the company may get into deep trouble. The Enron and WorldCom scandals of the early 2000s were clear examples of leaders who wanted to hit record-high profits at all costs, but ended up destroying their companies. Lack of cybersecurity in order to save money is another clear example of exposing a company's assets, employee records, or private customer information.

- Satisfying customers has always been one of the top objectives for companies. But again, if that comes at a cost of putting them in danger, then the goal is to protect them first before addressing their needs. The Boeing 737 MAX 8 was better and faster but not safer. So, while that aircraft was supposed to make customers happy by enabling them to reach their destination faster and cheaper, its faulty design actually ended up causing two airplane crashes in 2018 and 2019. The crashes resulted in tragic deaths and grief, but also caused massive negative implications for the manufacturer, which made trying to remedy the situation and regain customers' trust very difficult.

- Protecting employees should also be a priority for company leaders. Not only is this protection physical, by ensuring a safer work environment and following proper protocols, but it also has to do with operations. In other words, the processes that employees go through must also comply with standards, regulations, laws, and acceptable practices. For example, bribes and expensive gifts should be banned—even though they may get a deal done and satisfy shareholders, the aftermath and consequences of those practices could cause the employees to lose their jobs, be imprisoned, or muddy their public reputation. It can also cause the company to be fined or banned from operating in certain jurisdictions.

- Ensuring that the community is protected is another critical element to address while operating any business. Being responsible citizens regarding the planet and environment helps improve the ecological elements that ensure we, including future generations, all live in better, safer environments. Using environmentally friendly materials and reducing carbon dioxide, energy consumption, and global warming as well as increasing green space are only a few examples of what individuals and organizations can do to support a better planet.

3

What Should We Do Now?

Theodore Roosevelt said, "In any moment of decision, the best thing you can do is the right thing, the next best thing is the wrong thing, and the worst thing you can do is nothing."[3]

Many would argue that it is harder for big organizations to adapt to change than small ones. Think of a business like a ship: it is more difficult for big ships to change their course than smaller ones, which can be nimble and swift. The solution for big companies in coping with this issue and having lesser change resistance is to enable small incremental changes, and quickly. The wrong thing to do is to enable change but not fast enough, so that competitors find their way to the target first. The worst thing to do is nothing.

Jump out of the steady state while you still have strength. The boiling frog syndrome metaphor suggests that if a frog is put suddenly into boiling water, it will jump out, but if the frog is put in warm water then brought to a boil slowly, it will not perceive the danger and will be cooked to death. People are usually unwilling to react to or be aware of threats that arise gradually rather than suddenly. While some may argue that the frog might jump out of water even if the pot is gradually heated, the point is that when their business is in a comfortable, steady state, companies may not be able or willing to react to a changing environment when the change happens slowly. They do not usually feel the threat or realize the danger until it is too late to jump out of it.

Businesses should encourage out-of-the-box thinking and find opportunities to get out of situations when markets or profits are being eroded. Every company has its own environment that mandates certain strategies and tactics that could work at a certain time in a certain place based on a complicated mix of variables. It is critical to exploit disruptive forces and find solutions and opportunities in current or different markets. The solution can be as simple as tweaking an offering or as complicated as reinventing the company's DNA.

THE MARKET DOMINANCE QUADRANT

The challenge for any company in becoming a market leader and staying that way is developing, building, and implementing a winning strategy. Those who can first sense the disruption will gain an opportunity to drive it, shape their industry to embed it, and potentially capture rewards. The strategy will be different based on the organization's spot in the Market Dominance quadrant and depending on whether the company is a market leader, challenger, follower, or nicher.

Market leader: The company that is dominant in its industry with the biggest market share, customer base, distribution channels, and usually the most profit. A market leader is more than capable of developing new, innovative products and services with the guidance of long-term-focused leaders. Protecting the turf and market share is one way to maintain existence, but continuous improvement, expanding into other markets, and developing new offerings while improving customer service is the best winning strategy. Examples of market leaders: Toyota in automobiles, Unilever in consumer goods, Coca-Cola in soft drinks, and McDonald's in fast food.

Market challenger: Usually a company that has a strong presence but not a dominant position. Its strategy usually is trying to follow the leader and gain market share. The challenger finds opportunities in the market that can specialize on and differentiate products or services to address certain needs and create values, while the leader is busy looking after its own market. The challenger may offer extensions to certain products the market leader has or develop new products with different quality standards and prices. Examples of market challengers: Hyundai in automobiles, Procter & Gamble in consumer goods, PepsiCo in soft drinks, and Burger King in fast food.

Market follower: The "play it safe" company that tries to copy or develop similar products or services offered by the leader and challenger. It usually tries to penetrate market share with little risk and no investment in innovation. The follower tries not to fight the leader and challenger in open field but rather focuses on targeted marketing strategies that are less expensive. Examples of market followers: Tesla was a follower but is now a leader in the automobile industry, Kellogg's or Kraft Heinz in consumer foods, Keurig Dr Pepper in soft drinks, and Wendy's in fast food.

Market nicher: A company that concentrates on a select few target segments and focuses marketing efforts on one or two narrow market segments. The nicher tailors the marketing mix to better meet the needs of that target market. Examples of market nichers: Lamborghini in automobiles, Mars in consumer goods, Red Bull in soft drinks, and Del Taco in fast food.

ORGANIZATION GROWTH STRATEGIES

Below are strategies that can be adopted by companies no matter where they sit in the Market Dominance quadrant. Everything depends on the variables and circumstances at a certain time in a certain place, and one or more strategies can apply. It is worth mentioning again that this book provides only highlights to inform and remind the reader of such strategies. Each one of the following topics has advantages and disadvantages. In fact, there are many publications and books that go into much more detail about each strategy. These strategies are not mutually exclusive, as some organic and inorganic strategies can impact, enable, or complement each other.

Organic Growth

Organizations choose to expand output by targeting internal activities that increase revenue and reduce cost. Organic growth is usually limited and slower than inorganic growth due to the lack of resources. Also, if the industry has relatively high inorganic activity, then the competitors may also be exploring inorganic growth that might allow them to grow quicker and gain competitive edge.

Increase volume sold in the market: If the market has capacity or it is not fully exploited by the organization and its competitors, then this would be a good option, provided that the organization has the capacity and can meet the high demand. Increasing volume sold in the market would need significant marketing efforts and can be achieved through one of the following strategies:

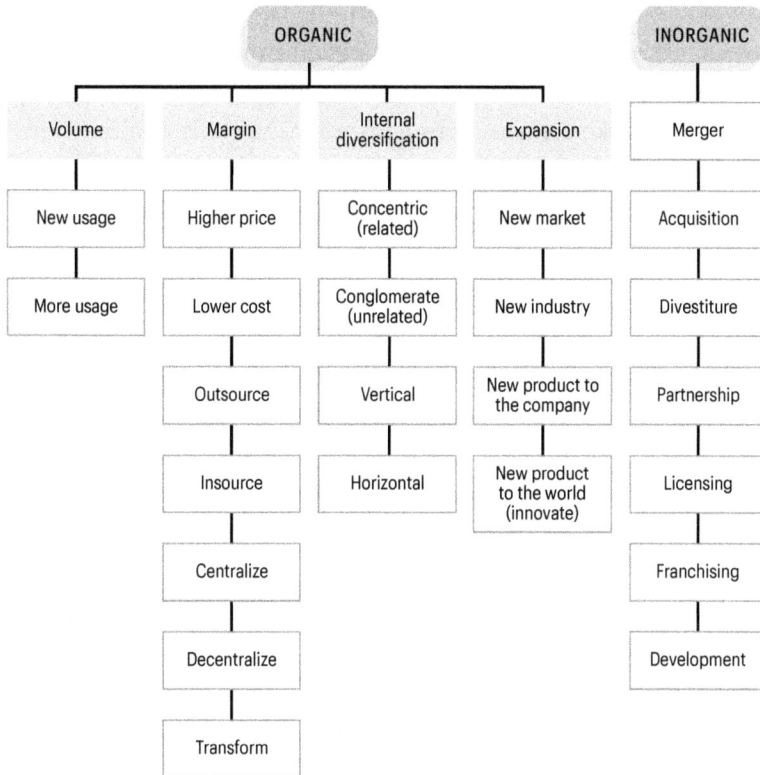

- **New usage:** In addition to attracting new customers to buy products or services, companies may try to find new ways to use those offerings. For example, WD-40 was designed with the intention of displacing and repelling standing water in order to prevent corrosion in nuclear missiles. New usages by customers include lubricating joints and hinges, removing dirt, and loosening stuck screws and bolts. Another example is the relatively new, increased popularity of cannabidiol (aka CBD) oil, to treat pain and anxiety (this active ingredient is derived from the hemp plant but creates a spectrum of usage beyond what cannabis was initially known for).

- **More usage:** Educate current customers on the benefits of using more of the organization's products, which means buying and consuming more. An example would be a yogurt company educating customers on the benefits of yogurt and how it contains calcium, vitamin D, and probiotics, then encouraging them to consume more per day than they are used to. Another example would be protein bar or protein shake companies bringing more awareness of the importance of protein and how many grams people need to consume per day to sustain or increase their muscle strength and size.

Margin: In business, margin is simply the difference between gross sales and cost of goods/services sold, expressed as a percentage of sales revenue. It can be improved by increasing sales and/or decreasing cost. By increasing margin, organizations will have more cash flow that can be utilized in several ways such as paying debt, distributing dividends to shareholders, investing in marketing efforts to increase sales, or developing new products and services.

- **Higher price:** One way to increase profitability is to increase prices where and when applicable. Of course, customers do not always appreciate price increases, but sometimes this action is necessary or just common sense. For instance, a company may not be able to absorb inflation costs and may need to transfer some of those costs to customers, especially when competitors are doing the same.

An organization may already be operating at full capacity with little to no inventory while enjoying strong customer demands. In this case, it is generally an easy decision to systematically increase prices while keeping an eye on competitors and demand impact. Think of how Apple and Samsung have been increasing the prices of their new flagship phones every year while watching each other to make sure they can stay competitive.

- **Lower cost:** Most of the time, companies cannot simply increase the prices of their products and services because of competitive pressure or regulatory mandates. The most common strategy in today's business environment is to find ways to do the same job or offer the same products and services as competitors, but faster, better, and cheaper. Lowering cost means increasing efficiency and productivity. Tackling cost means that leaders need to look at every cost item, direct and indirect, in the financial statements. Organizations can go back to their providers and suppliers to renegotiate and lower the prices they pay for raw materials and services. They can also try to find alternative sources or better and cheaper sources for their input cost. This can be achieved by getting requests for quotes (RFQs) and requests for proposals (RFPs) and comparing available options from vendors. If companies have debt, they may look for alternative funding options to lower the interest rates they pay. Labor cost is definitely one of the biggest input costs, so businesses should explore automation, robotics, and self-serve options, as well as find ways to increase employees' productivity through training, improving the work environment, and tying wages directly or indirectly to performance.

- **Outsource:** Typically, companies that operate in advanced countries and specific metropolitan areas have higher production costs than those in other, less-developed countries or locations. High office rent, wages, taxes, and other direct and indirect costs put pressure on organizations to look for alternative solutions in order to stay competitive. There are usually other providers that can produce parts or all of a company's offerings at a lesser cost. Maybe these suppliers are specialized in certain areas, and have become very efficient in doing that work, and offer the service or products faster, better, and cheaper. Examples include hotels outsourcing laundry or housekeeping, or organizations outsourcing certain functions like HR, accounting, or IT. Maybe those suppliers are located in countries or geographic areas that are cheaper, have less restrictions, and may have already established trade agreements that offer easy import and export of fully or partially produced products. The accelerated advancement in technology, communication, and transportation has made outsourcing work very common over the past two decades. Examples are outsourcing call centers, web designers, and software engineering from the United States and Europe to India, Malaysia, Indonesia, and other countries, or outsourcing computer chips and LCD screens to South Korea and China.

- **Insource:** Sometimes reversing the outsourcing module is a company's best strategy. This is true if the organization finds ways to do the job safer, cheaper, better, or faster than its suppliers. It could be the case that the suppliers are not continuously meeting the safety standards that the company, its customers, or its regulators are seeking, and the company may then regain control to ensure its reputation is not at risk. Sometimes a company can find ways to do its job cheaper through advanced technology or lowering labor and production costs. There are many examples of companies missing sales opportunities because of non-local suppliers' turnaround time. Businesses simply need to be faster to market in order to be competitive, and it is best then to do the work locally and closer to their customers if that is economically feasible. Governments sometimes give incentives for businesses to insource or move their operations locally versus internationally, and companies should capitalize on those opportunities if the numbers make sense.

- **Centralize:** When a company expands and has several locations or operating units, it may be time to think about centralization. Many organizations enjoy a very healthy margin by creating a "shared services" structure, where they create centralized HR, Finance, Marketing, IT, call center, customer service, research and development, and other departments that support all or some locations and units. For example, for a company that has tens or hundreds of locations, it might be easier and more efficient to have a corporate structure where those providing administrative work can support all or some locations and units instead of hiring one or more administrative employees per department (HR, Finance, IT, etc.) in each unit. The savings can be massive, and the process can be standardized. Allocating the cost of those shared services to each location or unit can be established based on different criteria.

- **Decentralize:** While centralization has been very common in recent years to benefit from lower cost and high margin, some organizations claim that it can also produce a high level of bureaucracy and frustration. Complaints regarding centralization include complicated organizational structure, slow execution, puzzling processes, and slower response to market change. Decentralization can offer a strategy that some organizations might want to explore in case their centralized structure is unsuccessful. Decentralization would give power back to the operating units to enable them to make decisions quickly and operate their units like solo entrepreneurs.

However, by allowing decentralization, companies may be exposed to a slew of issues such as disjointed technology, unstructured processes, varied cultures within a culture, non-streamlined processes, and no economies of scale when negotiating prices with vendors.

- **Transform:** Business transformation can have a spectrum of possibilities that range from simple changes in process, product, or service to complicated digital transformation and even a whole organizational DNA transformation in culture, structure, mission, vision, and values. Think about the following examples of transformation: Netflix went from online video content streaming to creating its own contents and programming. Netflix did not really change its DNA but transformed its operation to fit customer demand. Other companies have transformed their whole core and become market leaders. Think about Apple's transformation from solely a computer retailer to also a major smartphone and cloud provider, or how Amazon moved from a simple online bookstore to a comprehensive online retailer and cloud computing provider.

Internal diversification: Simply put, it means adding products, services, or stages of production or service to the existing business. This allows an organization to add lines of business to their current offerings. It also assumes that the company has the resources and capacity to extend its offering and better utilize their resources and knowledge.

- **Concentric (related):** Companies can add new offerings related to their existing lines of business. This strategy usually allows a company to realize synergies and expand reach, and maybe expand into businesses with different seasonal or cyclical sales patterns. Usually this strategy helps reverse declining sales in one product with another product that is related in nature. An example would be a company producing ice skates and roller blades—one product line's demand increases in winter while the other expands in summer.

- **Conglomerate (unrelated):** Businesses can add new products or services that have no common relationship with their existing lines of business. This serves as a diversification opportunity to capture new markets and utilize existing experience in expanding new products and services. Examples would be Alphabet investing in cloud and web hosting in addition to Google's search engine, Samsung investing in ships and construction in addition to electronics, and Disney investing in theme parks in addition to film production.

- **Vertical:** Firms can expand operations at different stages of production or service. This can be through developing these capabilities inside the company or acquiring another company. A common vertical diversification practice is changing from buying raw materials and producing finished products to producing both raw materials and finished products. An example would be a company that buys steel billets to produce rebar changing and expanding to produce both billets and rebar; this is called Backward Diversification. Alternatively, a company offering wholesale can expand its operations to retail; this is called Forward Diversification.

- **Horizontal:** Organizations can, of course, enter new business (related or unrelated). Examples would be a clothing company starting to sell shoes (concentric), or a plumbing company beginning to offer heating and cooling services (conglomerate). Companies utilizing this strategy benefit from efficiency and utilizing existing facilities and resources to create value through their new products or services.

Expansion: Organizations use this strategy to explore areas outside of their current operations to find access to new offerings, markets, or even industries.

- **New market:** Simply put, this is when companies expand into new territories, such as offering services and products in international markets. Barriers of entry can be very high in certain markets, so the path to success in this venture is definitely not rosy. Tariffs, competition retaliation, cultural differences, and laws and regulations are just a few factors that can present serious challenges while entering new markets. Target entering the Canadian market is a well-known new market entry failure.

- **New industry:** General Electric was famous for entering new industries. While its core business encompasses energy, aviation, lighting, and manufacturing, the organization did enter into a wide variety of new industries such as health care, finance, insurance, fleet services, oil and gas, and television and broadcasting. While branching out into new industries can be a great strategy to diversify products and services and expand an organization's reach, it can quickly cause issues such as a loss of focus on the firm's core business. There are many success and failure stories in the business world of companies that did and didn't execute this strategy well. Microsoft lost millions of dollars trying to enter the smartphone operating system world and could not move the needle against powerful industry giants like Samsung and Apple.

- **New product to the company:** Companies may try to increase their products and services mix by introducing new products. One success story is Google's introduction of the Chrome browser, a new product that quickly became dominant in the market. They were also successful in introducing Gmail and, later, the G Suite. However, Google has also experienced failure in launching new products, as was the case with Google+ or Google Glass, due to the product's imperfections, bugs, and privacy concerns.

- **New product to the world:** Breakthrough innovation comes in two forms: a new business model that utilizes existing technology or new technology that is based on an existing business model. An example of a successful business model is the Dollar Shave Club, a company that offers subscription-based products and service, delivering fresh razors to its customers every four weeks for a dollar. In less than five years, the company was sold to Unilever for $1 billion after reaching over 3.2 million members. Of course, there are countless examples of failed innovation as well, from New Coke to Windows Vista to Lululemon's Astro Pants.

Inorganic Growth

This also can be labeled as "External Diversification." Firms may choose to grow inorganically in new markets through strategies such as successful M&As. Compared to organic growth, inorganic growth is usually a faster way for a company to grow. When an inorganic expansion happens, an organization gains more assets, a greater customer base, and market share. On the flip side, restructuring costs and integration can greatly increase expenses. It could mean layoffs and changes in leadership teams, which could present challenges to sustaining knowledge and human capital. Most inorganic strategies take a long time from inception through completion, ranging from months to years, and could depend on many factors, including time for due diligence and regulatory filing. However, those strategies can still be faster than organic attempts to enter new markets, increase capabilities, and realize competitive advantage.

It is important to reemphasize that any of the inorganic strategies listed below can and should enable one or more of the strategies discussed in the Organic section, including Volume, Margin, Diversification, and Expansion.

- **Merger:** Two or more separate organizations can combine forces to create a new joint entity. Typically, a merger occurs when the businesses are about the same size and mutually agree to become equal partners in the new venture. The objective of the merger is usually to increase market share, improve economies of scale, achieve synergies, increase sales, and boost capabilities.

- **Acquisition:** Simply put, acquisition is when one organization takes over another. Sometimes the purchase is friendly, and sometimes it is hostile. Generally, the bigger firm assumes control of assets and management and keeps its name. Sometimes, the smaller firm acquires management control of the larger company and retains the name of the latter for the new, combined entity. This is referred to as a reverse takeover. Acquisition also attempts to increase market share, enter into new markets, achieve synergies, and boost capabilities.

While M&As seem attractive, and they may very well be sometimes the right strategy, according to the *Harvard Business Review*, studies show that between 70 and 90 percent of M&As fail to achieve their perceived value.[4] This could be because the wrong companies are purchased for the wrong purpose, the wrong measures of value are applied in pricing the deals, and the wrong elements are integrated into the wrong business models.

- **Divestiture:** A divestiture is the disposal of a business unit or subsidiary through closure, bankruptcy, or selling off exchange. Organizations may need to get rid of certain business or subsidiaries to obtain cash that could be valuable in investing in its other businesses. They may move to divest in order to buy other types of businesses and complement their existing line of products when assets are not performing well because they are not part of the core offerings, or when the divest business market is shrinking and the company wants to exit that line of business. Organizations may also divest to exit a certain geographic market.

- **Partnership:** There are different types of partnerships, but in general, partnership means an arrangement between two or more entities to oversee a business or operation while sharing profits and liabilities. Partnership can be very beneficial if done right. It is important to have good partnership agreements that detail how the business will operate, how profits and losses will be distributed, how decisions are made, how disputes are resolved, and how to exit safely in case the partnership fails.

- **Licensing:** This is an arrangement wherein one company gives another permission to manufacture or use its products and services for a specified fee. This strategy can be beneficial to both the licensee and licensor. The licensee can earn easy money while engaging in an asset-light relationship. Licensing gives the licensor quick access to markets and provides instant utilization of existing trademarks, brands, technology, distribution, and marketing systems that the licensee may have spent years building. Licensing fees typically amount to a small percentage of the gross or net sales.

- **Franchising:** Franchising is similar to licensing but a little more advanced; in fact, it is not always easy to distinguish between the two. The key difference is that franchising does not enable firms to make income from intellectual property owned by the franchisor (owner). Instead, the franchisor controls the brand and licenses the franchisee to use its successful business model and brand. In exchange, the franchisee invests capital for the business, operates the franchise, and pays a franchise fee. The franchisor generally has the ability to control how the business is run to maintain quality standards offered to customers. Meanwhile, the franchisor provides the franchisee with support in training, processes, best practices, marketing, and other tools needed to succeed in selected markets. Franchising is another great way for organizations to scale their business once it has proved to be successful, growing, and sustainable.

- **Development:** Some business development strategies can be organic but a strategy can also be inorganic such as when a firm raises capital and builds a business case to expand its businesses by developing new opportunities, venues, facilities, capabilities, or clients, and thereby drives growth outside of the normal course of business.

LEVERAGE PROVEN TECHNOLOGIES

Companies use advanced technologies to create value with less effort and find new ways to please customers. Whether the strategies of organizations are organic or inorganic, technology plays a pivotal role in enabling those strategies and realizing competitive advantage to increase efficiency and boost customer experience.

The following are key elements to address in order to successfully leverage digital transformation and capture values while aligning with business strategies.

Innovate and take educated risks: Companies should always seek a competitive advantage, and most of the time, this comes with innovations in processes and technologies. However, organizations will want to avoid presenting suboptimal digital solutions to customers because this can tarnish their reputation and jeopardize their credibility. It is fine to iterate solutions and seek customer input, but companies should disclose this approach and also ensure the technology is safe. Organizations do not need lawsuits caused by a data breach or injuries from technology; these issues bring on financial trouble and dents in a company's reputation that are difficult to reverse.

Power scalable digital solutions that work: Many organizations try to leverage technology-enabled models to update or replace their legacy systems while enabling a technology transformation that works. Often the journey to complete those digital transformation efforts is long and rocky because existing sticky processes need to be broken and redesigned, new systems and solutions need to be put in place, and people are expected to change the way they do their work to adapt to the new technologies. The problem appears when solutions that are put in place do not work as designed, causing wasted effort and money. For example, many times, IT leaders fail to align with business leaders on requirements needed to be built into the systems. Also, because the journey is too long, the people who design or sponsor it end up moving into different roles or to different organizations, leaving many questions as to why certain solutions were put in place or designed a certain way. By the time transformation is complete, there could be a whole new technology that renders the current one obsolete. It is important to ensure the alignment of IT and other business functions in designing the digital transformation road map, and that not only do those technologies work for current needs, but also they are able to be upgraded easily to meet future requirements.

Create new ways to please customers: Technology transformations are ultimately created to help meet or exceed the expectations of existing and new customers. According to Gartner (gartner.com), more than 125,000 enterprises launched digital transformation initiatives in 2016 expecting to increase their revenue by more than 80 percent by 2020.[5] Increasing revenue comes from attracting new customers and upselling existing customers. Over the years, there have been many examples of companies that managed to provide their customers with cutting-edge technology that surprised and delighted them. Some popular examples include Tesla, Apple, and Salesforce. In less than ten years, and through proven innovative technology, Tesla managed to attract and please its customers in such a way that in early 2020, the company achieved a market value that now surpasses that of century-old powerful industry giants such as Ford and General Motors—combined.[6]

Increase value with less effort: Technology is also meant to increase efficiency. It can accomplish that by either speeding up existing processes or creating new, more efficient ones. Technology can significantly boost the productivity of the workforce by improving communication across the business (systems with systems, people with people, or people with systems), allow for faster data processing or retrieval, and introduce automation, which can reduce errors and the need for manual work.

Avoid increasing technical debt: Technical debt can result from rework caused by using shortcuts while developing technology solutions, instead of doing it right the first time, which is usually a result of prioritizing speed over proper delivery. It can also result from unnecessary technical complexity through changes done by several people who do not understand the original design. Technical debt can be avoided by focusing on driving rapid changes and prioritizing speedy delivery while ensuring things are done right and that teams are not cutting corners. Rework can be costly and frustrating to customers and employees.

Focus on what matters: New technologies these days fall under many categories, such as automation, cloud use, blockchain, 5G networks, Internet of Things (IOT), machine learning (ML), artificial intelligence (AI), augmented reality (AR), and virtual reality (VR). The biggest challenge that business and IT leaders face is the huge number of technology solutions available and needed to transform their organizations. It is difficult to make decisions with regard to which technical solution is best and who would be the system integration partner to help implement them. Many times, there is no way back once decisions are made. Therefore, it is extremely important to have perfect alignment between business functions and IT to adequately focus on what really matters for the company and its customers. Sometimes, the leaders fall in the trap of doing too many things at the same time. Probably one of the most common reasons for failure in any digital transformation is overloading the effort with too many initiatives that can stretch thin the financial, technical, and human resources. It is also important to decide on what solutions are suitable for the current and upcoming business expansion plans, what support system integrators can offer, and which technology solution providers have their own road map for digital transformation that show continued innovation and investment in technological advancement.

Have an achievable harmonized digital road map: A clear and solid technical road map is extremely important to achieving the technology transformation vision. Depending on the organization, its technical structure, financial situations, and market conditions, the road map can have several phases. Some companies prefer to have a short-term investment in legacy systems until a fully comprehensive new digital solution is available. Others favor "ripping and replacing" those older systems and implementing the latest technologies. That scope then needs to be broken down into several steps along the road map to create a powerful tool that aligns the sequence of solutions to be developed, the approximate investment needed, and the time frame required to complete this journey. This road map must be built by closely collaborating efforts between business functions and IT while keeping a customer-centric mindset.

Build internal talent: Building and maintaining winning technologies requires trained, skillful, and capable technical people. Building in-house capabilities and attracting fine technology talent to deliver advanced technologies should be a priority when investing in digital transformation. Those resources should also be able to not only establish a modern technology environment but also drive the development of new solutions. Having sufficient technical talent is vital for the success of any business that wants to leverage technology as a competitive advantage.

4

Where Should We Focus?

I t is never too late for organizations to look for opportunities to sustain or grow their business organically or inorganically. The key terms here are "sustain" and "grow." In a declining economy, it is usually hard to grow business, so the focus is often on sustainability, whereas in a stable and growing economy, sustaining is not enough because, by default, if everyone else is growing and one firm is not, then it is falling behind quickly.

SWOT ANALYSIS

Where the focus should start probably depends on many variables and factors that organizations need to evaluate. It is recommended that businesses start evaluating what's "in the box" before looking "outside the box." In other words, organizations should look first into their internal capabilities, structures, financial health, advantages, disadvantages, opportunities, and threats.

Putting together a SWOT (strengths, weaknesses, opportunities, threats) analysis is a good idea, as it can help a business uncover opportunities that are up for grabs while trying to understand the weaknesses that can be scaled down or eliminated. It can also identify opportunities that an organization may or may not have thought of while highlighting threats that could hinder the company's efforts. The SWOT matrix is often a reflection of an internal-external matrix, as many see strengths and weaknesses as internal factors while opportunities and threats are external.

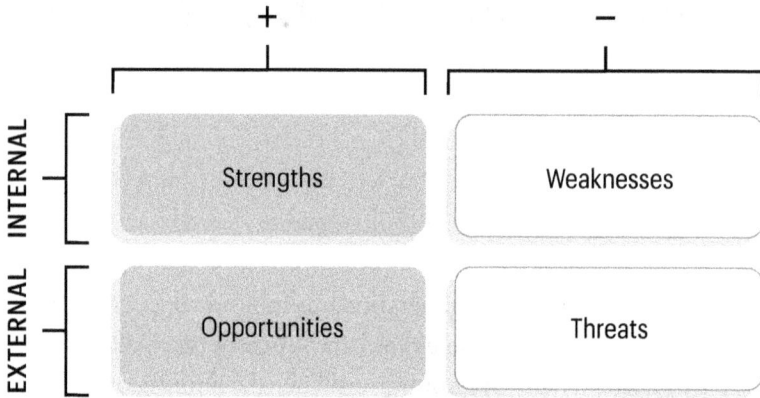

Internal Factors

Strengths: It is important to first evaluate the organization's positive capabilities that could be a competitive advantage in the marketplace. What exactly does the company do better than most or all other companies? Is the strength primarily in people, process, technology, brand, location, trademark, and/or data? Are the team members more trained, educated, and skilled, and do they have a better work ethic than other competitors? Are the processes and technologies that the company has implemented in complete harmony and do they provide significant tailwinds in any endeavor the company approaches? Maybe the company has unique sources of raw materials or supplies that the competition cannot easily access. Maybe it has a strong brand or patents backed by unique products or offerings that customers value. It is critical to do this analysis in a subjective way and separate from emotional attachment to the company and its offerings. Leaders can easily miss the mark if their vision is fogged by emotions or ego. They need to look at how customers and people in the market really view the company's offerings and how that compares to what their competitors are doing.

Weaknesses: Looking at weaknesses objectively is critical to understanding which areas an organization should focus on improving. Does the company have inferior products and services, or are the problems in the processes that get it out the door to customers? Does it have old technology that is not capable of handling customer demands or internal production efficiently? Is it the location, brand name, capabilities, or financial status? Maybe it is the leadership mindset that is myopic and not strategic. Whatever the weaknesses are, the healthiest thing for a business to do is face them and find solutions rather than sweep them under the rug. What really matters is what a company is doing about its weaknesses. Set strategies, tactics, milestones, and measurable objectives that address each suboptimal area the firm can identify. Some companies have managed to turn their weaknesses into strengths. Walmart, for example, managed to address its online ordering weakness and become a strong driver in the online retail space.

External Factors

Opportunities: If a firm digs for opportunities, it will find them. The question is whether or not the organization is putting in enough effort to discover those opportunities. Setting up market indicators, surveys, and research may be the easy part. The real traction starts by having the right resources to look into the data collected, find the opportunities, and then pass along the recommendations to the leaders. Then those company leaders can take the information and convert it into action. Pertinent information to examine for opportunity could contain market trends, customer behavior changes, social media feedback, technology that could complement or add to existing architecture, market demographic changes, income and life priority changes, expanding into markets and segments that are not serviced, and so on. Organizations should be willing to take calculated risks and ignite the out-of-the-box thinking in finding opportunities.

Threats: Any threat has the potential to weaken an organization. Companies do not exist in a vacuum. Competitors, small and big, are typically doing what they can to sustain and expand their markets and offerings. Organizations should always monitor threats and have mitigation plans ready to be activated should any of those threats materialize and start directly or indirectly impacting the business. Threats can come from obstacles that companies face in their current operation or may be from new business. Watching competitors closely can be a good tactic to ensure the company continues to be proactive and reactive to any competition development. Changes in technology are becoming faster and more impactful than ever. Keeping an eye on suppliers is also important, as they may raise their prices, run short on providing supplies, or even go out of business. Probably one of the most important areas to watch is customer behavior. Changing consumer behavior, such as switching to other markets, products, or services, can, of course, negatively impact business. Changes in political policies or economic status may also pose significant threats to the firm's strategies and tactics.

Analyzing internal and external factors through a SWOT matrix can guide organizations toward the right strategies while avoiding other ones that would likely be unsuccessful.

5

Whom Should We Target?

Organizations easily fall into a trap by assuming they know their customers and that those customers are loyal to the business' products and services. In today's environment, firms need to leave their ego at the door and realize that markets and customers are moving targets and need continual and proactive pulse checks on changes in needs and preferences. Changes in market and customer behavior are becoming frequent. Companies lose their edge when they lose focus on their customers.

It is vital to always listen to customers, understand their needs, and address every step in their journey of identifying, selecting, using, and repeating their purchase. Analyzing customer behavior gives leaders an idea of what triggers customers to pay for a firm's products or services, what their priorities are, and what can alter their purchase decision.

Having a customer-centric mindset allows for organizations to focus on always tying their actions to whatever makes customers happy. What should keep business leaders up at night is how to make improvement in every step throughout the customer journey.

CUSTOMER JOURNEY

The customer journey analyzes the steps customers take when they engage to obtain a service or product. Among a company's top priorities is knowing its customers and understanding their motives. Understanding the customer journey goes beyond the purchase of a product or service.

The following steps address the path customers usually take during their journey of identifying, acquiring, and potentially repeating or recommending a product or service. It is crucial that organizations understand what their customers are doing at each point in the six-step journey and what actions they are taking to move on to the next stage.

Need/want and awarness
Research and consideration
Purchase and fulfillment
Return and retention
Dispose and repeat
Promote and advocate

1. Need/want and awareness: The consumer's journey starts with a desire that is triggered by what they need or want. A customer's needs can be basic items like food, drinks, clothing, and shelter. What a customer wants may be an extension of a basic need, such as fancy food, luxury clothing, expensive homes, and so on. What customers want can be something they do not need but are enticed to acquire because of an awareness or interest triggered by something such as brochures, direct mail, banners, online advertisement, email, word of mouth, articles, reviews, and blogs.

Organizations should continuously use data analytics and market research to understand customer behavior and changes that trigger needs, and make sure they are using the right media channels while measuring those channels' impact. A key indicator might be in establishing a media impact score by asking customers where they found a product or heard about a service.

2. Research and consideration: After customers realize that they need or want something, they are most likely going to do some research to understand details about the product or service they want; they may read reviews or blogs, ask questions, try to understand purchasing mechanisms, shipping, delivery speed, and return policies, and compare with other products or services in the market.

Businesses' best advocate for their products and services is word of mouth from customers who have tried and liked their offerings. That can be as simple as previous customers talking about those products and services to friends or posting reviews online. Ratings are now available via apps, websites, agencies, and forums. BBB, Yelp, Amazon, Google, Facebook, and Tripadvisor are only a few examples of what is used by customers to post good or bad reviews. A glowing review would likely encourage potential customers to consider placing an order; a bad review may repel them.

3. Purchase and fulfillment: This stage is the most important in the customer journey. It is the moment of truth. It is what all the branding and marketing investment has been leading to. So, companies should make it count! Customers should find products or services quickly. They should be able to place an order or buy what they want easily and feel comfortable that their information is secure when they pay for products and services. Easy ordering platforms, visually pleasing displays, and pleasant customer service are all key factors in a customer's decision to make a purchase. Companies may want to focus on the customer experience especially at this stage. Customers need to feel that the transition is very smooth and easy. Picking a product or service, placing an order, shipping, tracking, delivery, and a satisfaction survey are steps that should be seamless to customers. If a product or service is offered in a retail environment, then customer courtesy and a comfortable shopping environment should also be added as areas of focus. Firms should establish key performance indicators (KPIs) to measure satisfaction scores at every step of a purchase to ensure smooth and easy transactions.

4. Return and retention: Depending on the product or service, customers may consume, use, retain, or return the item they purchased. At this point, customers usually care about the quality they get compared to the quality they expect. Does the item or service they bought exceed or meet their expectations or not? Once a product or service is purchased, customers look into things such as quality expectations, instructions for usage and access, how to find information needed online, ease of reaching customer service, and so on. Firms should also focus on their credibility by making return processes easy and clear. Losing customer trust can mean a loss of business. Establishing a return rate percentage and monitoring and responding to almost every customer review can put organizations on the right track to address any suboptimal experiences. Costco, for example, is widely known for its best-in-class customer experience, especially the return process. Many customers actually buy from Costco exclusively, to avoid the return hassle experienced when shopping at other retailers.

5. Dispose and repeat: Once the customers use the product or service, and presuming that they are happy with that experience, they may elect to repeat that purchase or add related accessories. This is the fruition of the customer journey, in the form of repeat customers. It is in a business' best interest to send offers to existing customers and/or create a loyalty program that earns customers points when they use a company's products and services. Bias aside, probably one of the best customer reward programs in business is the one by Caesars Entertainment. The Caesars Rewards program offers great benefits and rewards that keep customers happy and motivate them to return to Caesars properties again and again. It is a good idea for companies to establish a KPI to measure the frequent customer rate or repeat purchase rate. These rates enable companies to guide upcoming marketing efforts. If satisfied customers need to dispose of a product after use, they should not have any difficulty doing so. Although the customer may be satisfied with a product, if disposing it is unsafe or presents difficulties, then it could cause frustration and cost.

6. Promote and advocate: When customers are happy about a product or service they've purchased, and they are satisfied with their overall experience, they typically speak highly about it to friends and family. They may also post a review on a website, social media, or blog. They even often become the first to acquire new products and services from the same company as soon as they're on the market. A great example of a company that excels in customer loyalty is Apple. As soon as Apple launches a new version of the iPhone, customers line up for hours in the front of Apple stores to get their hands on it.

Companies should establish KPIs, such as a net promoter score (NPS) to monitor customer loyalty and advocacy on a regular basis. To ensure business sustainability, firms should focus on addressing any decline of that score.

Customers these days are more powerful than ever due to instant access to data and the power of online forums and social media. Customer loyalty is very hard to obtain and maintain nowadays, and it will be harder in the future. The new generations of customers are technically savvy and have far less brand loyalty than previous generations.

Therefore, organizations must always be on top of every aspect of customer behavior and changes in decision dynamics. They should establish and maintain comprehensive measurement of their customers' journey, and analyze and influence those customers dynamically and in real time as their behavior happens. Using IOT technology and advanced data analytics can help companies understand in real time why their customers are motivated to jump in and move from one stage to the next in the customer journey.

6

When Should
We Start Talking?

No company or industry is safe from business and technology disruption. The examples we see every day in the retail business are just the first wave of disruption impact. Brick-and-mortar business are now challenged by online and technologically advanced competitors.

The concept of business transformation is not new. IBM, for example, transformed its operations many times throughout its lifetime. Since IBM's founding in 1911, it has adapted and shaped its products and services over time to evolve and address the changes in customer demands. The challenge today is that the change is happening at a much-accelerated pace. Customers are demanding safer, better, faster, and cheaper products or services. They also have easy access to information, reviews, and competitors' offerings that are often efficient and innovative. So, if an organization is not moving fast and nimbly enough, it will likely fall far behind competitors that are able to meet the continued changes in customer demand.

The longer companies take to embrace change and transform their businesses, the harder it gets to sustain and grow. Sears, Charlotte Russe, Payless ShoeSource, Toys "R" Us, and Blockbuster are just a few companies that could not change fast enough to catch up. Tech companies have struggled as well; take for example Nokia, Yahoo!, RadioShack, Kodak, and BlackBerry. It is safe to say that most, if not all, of those companies tried to change in an effort to catch up with companies like Amazon, Netflix, Apple, and Google. The problem is, even if they wanted to and tried to change, they were not fast enough to make that change happen in their core business model to make a meaningful impact. Maybe the blame can be put on legacy systems or technical debt, but there are many other companies that not only maintained but also transformed their operations and offerings.

Some successful companies have elected to put some of their core products and services to sleep or sell them in order to reinvest in a growing and more promising business and technology. Walmart invested heavily in their supply chain system, grocery offerings, and online retail to reduce prices and offer home-delivery services. They did so in order to compete with other retailers such as Amazon, which bought Whole Foods to compete in the grocery market.

If companies of any size have not yet started looking for, investing in, and enabling change in their strategies to adopt optimization, innovation, or transformation, then they are probably late. So, to answer the question, "When should we start talking about transforming or optimizing our business?" the answer is "Yesterday!" Firms cannot keep their heads in the sand anymore. If feasible, organizations can consider engaging in partnerships with firms that can help them learn and innovate. If they do not have the experience and knowledge to transform their businesses, they can hire a business transformation specialist. They can adopt a proof-of-concept pilot and try launching new or complementary products and services in pilot markets to gauge customer reaction to those offerings.

Successful transformation or optimization requires C-suite support and a change management mindset among the leaders who cascade down to every level across the company. Today, there is no place for complacency in business. Launching into a multiyear transformation journey can feel overwhelming for many leaders, but the journey begins with one step. The important elements are will and action.

Also, it is crucial to note that leaders should adopt this effort not only for the sake of change, but also for the purpose of achieving meaningful change. Meaningful change adds real value to an organization and its shareholders, customers, employees, and future.

Industry disruption is reasonably predictable, but challenging the status quo is probably the hardest part of any change plan. Best practices of change management can be handy, especially at early stages, in order to drive collaboration and adoption. In postmortems, leaders often say that they should have started earlier. They also say that real meaningful change begins by identifying initiatives that add real value and build momentum with small incremental wins.

Communication is key, and I will address that component in many sections in this book and especially Part Three. Keep in mind that traditional one-way communication is not effective when making a change in an organization. Top-down communication is not enough to get the buy-in and support from employees. The senior management team should understand the need to change, but all employees in the organization should understand it as well. Two-way communication is vital in order to inspire confidence, gain support, and encourage engagement.

Some leaders try to use competition to drive the urgency of change. While this can be a good motive, it is wise for business leaders to search for their own need to change and seek opportunities whether triggered by competition or not. This can start with data and insights into where the company needs to be and when in order to sustain and grow its business. Leaders should be talking with their employees as soon as they start to form their concept of change. The smartest ideas sometimes come from the frontline workers, who are closer to the process and customers. Talking to employees as frequently as possible is a smart recipe for forming a good strategy, gathering the best ideas, getting buy-in and support, and driving meaningful change and nimble execution.

Here are questions that organization leaders can ask to understand what transformation strategy to pick, as well as when and where to pursue.

Questions about Customers

- Does the company know its customers (existing and potential)?

- Is the company focusing only on existing customers, or are efforts being made toward attracting new customers?

- Are current customers satisfied with what the company is offering them and how it is being offered?

- Is the company continuously losing customers? Does churn exist and at what rate?

- Does the company offer what customers truly need? And do the company's products or services satisfy those customers?

- Is the company focusing on the full customer experience and addressing every opportunity to fix gaps along the path in the customer journey?

- Does the company need more data to better understand who their customers are, what they want, what they need, how they are serviced, and how they perceive the company and its offerings?

Questions about Competitors

- What are competitors doing that the company is not?

- What can be done that competitors cannot easily replicate?

- What challenges are preventing the company from achieving competitive advantage today?

- Are new competition forces rising?

- From where are new competitors emerging, and how quickly?

- Are business barriers of entry getting lower by governments or because of globalization?

Questions about the Company

- What does the company have that can be exploited?

- What does the company lack that should be obtained to improve processes, data quality, products, services, technologies, or culture?

- How efficient and lean is the company?

- Are internal processes broken or bureaucratic?

- Is the company culture suitable for its industry?

- Can the company penetrate other industries or markets?

- How does the company fit into the community (local and cyber)?

- Does the company have a workforce that is ready to change and capable of changing?

Questions about Objectives

- What does success look like? Is the objective to survive? Is it to increase top line, bottom line, product/service variety, or gain market share?

- How can that success be measured?

- Can the company sustain that success?

7

How Are We Going to Change?

Now it is time to explore how to re-strategize the business and figure out the required tactics. It is important to tie every action to the company's holistic strategy. Japan has a good process that it began to use after World War II, called Hoshin Kanri. This method is currently utilized as part of Lean Six Sigma playbooks. Hoshin Kanri, or Policy Deployment, is a process that ensures that a company's strategic goals are being activated at every level within that company. We will not dive into the steps and methodology of Hoshin Kanri, but it is important to note that all the actions within the company from all levels should be tied to the organization's strategic objectives. This process will ensure that the resources are deployed properly and working on what really matters, which eliminates waste and confusion within an organization.

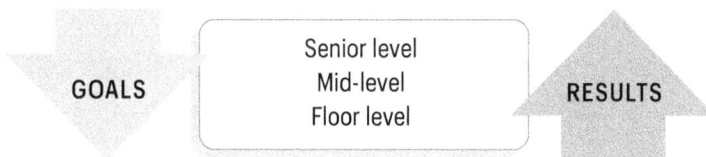

GOALS

Senior level
Mid-level
Floor level

RESULTS

THE TRANSFORMATION GOALS

In order to enable change in an organization, it is vital to remember that the process should be in the following order: safer, better, faster, smarter, and cheaper (maybe).

Safer: Safety is always first. No matter how much better, faster, smarter, or cheaper a company's products or services, if they are not safer, the company can easily lose money or, worse, its credibility. As outlined in chapter 2, safety is always the number one priority. Protecting the company, customers, employees, and community should always be a prerequisite and part of all organizations' DNA.

Better: Companies should always look for ways to make their products and services better in order to meet or exceed evolving customer demands. Fewer defects, better functionality, a more streamlined process, and higher service standards are examples of how a company can better position its offerings to customers. Sometimes "better" comes with a cost, as it may be easy to change a material or add a feature, but, arguably, companies may be able to offset these increased costs by finding cheaper sources or making their processes more efficient.

Faster: Time is money, so companies should continue to make efforts to deliver their products and services to their customers faster. However, faster does not always mean working harder or adding more resources; sometimes just adding resources and effort can create chaos and cause adverse results. Also, consider the law of diminishing returns, in which the level of benefits gained is less than the number of resources and amount of effort invested. Ways to boost speed include simplifying and streamlining the process, introducing automation, combining processes when applicable, utilizing technology, and increasing effective communication.

Smarter: We all need to work smarter, not only harder. Making a process easier would mean less time and effort spent to deliver an objective. Smarter means getting more done in the same amount of time without significantly adding more effort. Again, utilizing technology, better processes, and improved communication can lead to smarter business operating models.

Cheaper (maybe): In many cases, it is accurate to assume that customers expect cheaper products and services but not at the cost of quality. Maybe the competition is exerting pressure and products and prices are elastic with the demand, which means the lower the price, the more products or services can be sold. Companies usually struggle with reducing prices because they face increasing input costs such as labor, materials, inflation, and tariffs. Technology, AI, and automation are only a few examples of how organizations are able to deliver cheaper prices. Renegotiating with suppliers or finding alternative sources can also be solutions to reduce prices. Streamlining the production or service process is another possibility. However, I tacked "maybe" onto "cheaper" because customers may be fine with maintaining or increasing a product or service price if the company can justify that increase with better quality or options while highlighting the differentiation from competitive offerings. But if the products or services in the marketplace are homogenous, then competing in price may be the only way to win customers.

TYPES OF TRANSFORMATION

Business transformation is a change strategy that helps move an organization from a current state to a better future state by changing people, processes, and/or technologies. In many cases, a transformation effort to fundamentally and systematically move the company to a better state achieves the company's objectives and positively impacts the business. It is important to mention that transformation is generally a pivotal shift in strategies, processes, or technologies, whereas optimization refers to less drastic changes in those strategies, processes, or technologies.

As discussed in chapter 1, there are many reasons for a business to consider a transformation, including competition threats, shifts in customer priorities, new technologies, changes in market dynamics, increased input cost, or other external factors. Business transformation can take two main forms:

1. Functional transformation: Transformation may be specific in certain business verticals to seek higher efficiency and productivity. The objective is to do the job safer, better, faster, smarter, and potentially cheaper. Changes and improvement can be in business functions such as operations, finance, marketing, sales, supply chain, human resources, or research and development. This can also be referred to as "functional transformation." Change in technology is often referred to as "digital transformation." A common example would be migrating from legacy on-premise technology to cloud computing, or moving from a local financial system to a fully integrated enterprise resource planning (ERP) system, or even putting together a customer relationship management (CRM) system that combines all customer data and linking it to marketing campaigns and sale agents.

2. Total transformation: Transformation may involve changes to the entire organization—for example, transforming strategy to switch the direction of a company to a new focus, when integrating two entities within the same company, or even transforming the business as a result of a merge with or acquisition of another company. It is important to understand that when businesses go through the process of transformation and embracing change, the journey is not always going to be smooth and easy. Resilience, actions, keeping the pressure, transparency, and continued 360-degree communication are generally key for successful transformation. The rule of thumb is not to seek a short-term fix to a long-term problem. The best option here is to rip off the Band-Aid, avoid myopic thinking, and always be customer-centric.

TRANSFORMATION ROAD MAP

Although no business transformation is ever the same, the following is a guide to the steps of successful business transformation.

Chartering: Create a vision and evaluate at a high level why the company is thinking about transformation, what is triggering this effort, if it is a functional or total transformation, if there are internal resources and skills that can do the work or if there is a need for outsourced consultants and agencies, how much money should be set aside for this effort, approximately how long the journey will take, how life should look like after the transformation is complete, and if there will be a continued change mechanism in the future.

Form strategies and tactics: Create a clearly defined scope that aligns the new business case with the strategic goals of the organization and how that can be translated to shorter-term tactics that can then be streamlined to a new operating model. At this stage, it is the right time to map out the current state, the desired future state, any interim state, and risks and threats.

Set up a transformation leadership team: In order for a transformation effort to be effective, a charismatic and action-oriented leader has to lead that work frame and provide oversight and support. Also, that person should have direct access to the CEO and the executive leadership team. Even with all of the leadership traits this leader may have, without authority and power that cascades actions and pushes messages from the top down, the transformation efforts will go sideways and may never lead to fruition. The transformation leaders should then recruit the right team to help deliver the objectives of that effort.

Build a project management office (PMO): PMOs are utilized to establish governance and ensure that the efforts of the company are aligned and not duplicative, and that the teams involved are communicating and not stepping on each other's toes. You'll need to ensure that the initiatives are moving properly, from ideation to execution and closing without bottlenecks. Meanwhile, a tracker should be established to ensure a pulse check is applied frequently to know what is and is not working, and make any changes midcourse; all of that is part of the PMO objectives. It is advisable that the PMO be working across all functions to ensure it is not directly influenced by a single vertical, and at the same time have visibility to all initiatives in the organization to eliminate redundancies and align efforts. Cross-functional alignment is key to preventing impediment to the process. An empowered PMO is usually the perfect solution for that mandate. An enterprise project management office (EPMO) can also be a solid solution that operates at a strategic level in collaboration with an organization's executives. The goal of this centralized EPMO is to provide company-wide guidance, governance, standardized processes, and project portfolio management best practices, tools, and techniques.

Planning: Once the vision, strategy, and team are established, the company should develop a path forward to help achieve its objectives. Planning sets out who is doing what and when, what are the interdependencies, and how many resources are needed and when. Recently, there has been an industry-wide push toward less planning and more Agile methodology (involving a particular approach to project management typically used in software development) use that relies on small incremental deliverables with repeated sprints and retrospectives. That may work better for a product or software development work, but for big transformation, it is critical to establish clear objectives, a work-breakdown structure (WBS), milestones, a schedule, resources, and a budget. Planning for communication, training, and other change management best practices is also key to ensuring faster adoption to change by all stakeholders (employees, customers, stockholders, community, and so on).

Execution: After a holistic plan has been put in place, the team can start executing its objectives according to that plan. The plan is often not carved in stone, since things change along the way or early assumptions in the strategy may not align with the organization's path. This phase is by far the hardest part; the execution journey can be full of disappointment and resistance, but that is why resilience and action-oriented mindsets are key to keeping the pressure on, under the direction of a true charismatic leader who acts as change champion. Engaging stakeholders and communicating often is the secret recipe to succeeding in transforming any business. Also, having leaders from every functional vertical assigned to the transformational effort ensures that workstreams are represented and adds diverse skillsets to make effective change happen.

Tracking and validation: A tracker needs to be established to ensure that the transformation leaders regularly apply a pulse check so they understand what is working and what is not. Measuring improvement and keeping the transformation efforts on track can be overwhelming. Sometimes there are so many forces that impact a business that it is very hard to isolate the true impact of the transformation effort. Advanced analytics and financial planning and analysis (FP&A) can create dashboards and KPIs to measure the change impact. Validating assumptions along the way is critical so that directions can change before the team takes a path that could be hard to alter in the future. The team should establish a governance structure to report vertically and horizontally when applicable, establish a frequent communication rhythm, escalate any risks or issues, and take actions quickly when needed.

Operationalizing: While transformation can be continuous, there should be a point in time at which the future process or model is eventually put in place and is part of a new operating engine. Integrating the transformation initiatives into the new planned operating model is vital. Part of the transformational change management model is to ensure that integration with a new operational model happens.

LESSONS LEARNED FROM TRANSFORMATION EFFORTS THAT FAILED

The following are items that were identified during postmortems of many failed transformational efforts.

Weak sponsorship: Successful transformation needs change leadership and reinforcement. This requires a strong leader to sponsor and drive such transformation while inspiring the stakeholders involved. That person should also have authority and direct access to the C-suite. Lacking motivation, loss of focus, or unsupportive senior executives causes any business transformation to miss objectives.

Big errors in the strategy: Pursuing the wrong strategy can easily lead to drastic business transformation failure. Take for example Kodak's double down on Polaroid technology when digital photography was picking up speed. Seeking unproven technologies or implementing inconsistent practices that do not help scale the business are other examples of errors in strategy. Another failure point is targeting unrealistic goals, such as setting an insufficient time frame for the full implantation of a company's ERP transformation efforts.

Getting stuck in the past: Organizations may fail to change their mindset and switch to a new line of thinking. Resisting change can also be part of a company's culture. Sometimes the leaders of an organization unintentionally reject the brightest ideas and get stuck in their old way of thinking. The middle and line managers also may pull the company back into how it operated for years by not supporting change and not making meaningful efforts to adopt a new business model, instead committing themselves to the business death "sentence": "We have always done it this way!"

Leadership misalignment: Companies should anticipate resistance to change at different stages in the optimization and transformation journey. This resistance triggers misalignment, especially among the leadership team. Often the issues appear during a business' change process when moving from "what" to do into "how" teams should do it. During transformation, functions may disappear, jobs may change, roles may be created while others get eliminated, and authority status may move from one person to another. It is not always easy to let go, especially for leaders who have been with the company for a long time. The mindset should change from "this is what we think" to "this is what we all agreed to do." Transformation fails when different leaders start to give different directions. This happens when those leaders stop talking and trusting each other. A strong sponsor and C-suite will definitely help avoid this issue. Measuring alignment along the way through communication and governance plans (monthly, quarterly, qualitative, quantitative, and so on) is vital to transformation success; it allows leaders to act immediately when problems arise, to ensure no leakage can sink the ship during the transformation journey.

Poor change management: Business transformation is set for success when a company identifies the right people as stakeholders to champion the change. Following the implementation of any new system or process, there is an immediate drop in performance based on resistance and inertia. Companies can minimize the duration and depth of that performance drop by anticipating the change, planning for it, and proactively managing it. They can put organizational change management (OCM) best practices in place to make the journey smoother and reach the target sooner. Being clear on the future state of the operation and what roles and responsibilities are changing, and how to be prepared for the change are key to succeeding in the transformation effort. OCM will outline communication channels and streams. It will also help determine, without causing anxiety, if there is a skill gap moving to new business or technology, and if additional training is required to ensure confidence in the new business model. Missing OCM in any project can easily cause delays in reaching the end goal and in getting the results that are outlined in the business case. Change management will be addressed in more detail in Part Three of this book.

Not relying on data: Data will be a big section in Part Two of this book, but it is important to note here that data is not only powerful for any organization to utilize during business transformation, but also necessary. Companies should seek to become data-driven, and potentially hire data scientists and statisticians to create advanced analytics capabilities. In many cases, transformations require explanation to stakeholders as to why it is important and why certain initiatives have been prioritized. Without data that backs up every decision, change sponsors can appear as though they are guessing. Data will support the notion to challenge the status quo by showing certain trends in the market, correlation between behavior and volume, market or economic dynamics on product and market mix, and many more measures and analyses that support decision making versus gut feelings. If the change leaders are not demonstrating a data-driven decision-making process, they will not get support from the senior leaders or line workers.

Not paying attention to blind spots: It is easy for any business transformation team to get lost during the journey. It is common for organizations to face serious issues during the process of transformation simply because they missed checking their blind spots while trying to instigate positive change to their companies. Teams may linger too much on data analysis without taking action, or they may dance around their sweet spots without taking educated risks. Other times, they may become too stubborn and lack flexibility in iteratively changing their own path when needed. Not having the right stakeholders in the room or allowing for siloed activities may cause rework and redundancy.

Not being focused on what matters: Another common cause of transformational failure is overcomplicating the effort with too many initiatives at the same time. It is easy to get excited and ready to go for change, and leaders tend sometimes to overpromise, which can cause them to potentially underdeliver. Not having a clear business case allows for "scope creep" to happen, causing resources to be overconsumed for things that may not be important. Also, weak sponsors who agree on all the new ideas often cause the team to stretch themselves and potentially lose focus on what matters most. Tying the budget and resources to the initiatives and having a good tracker are best practices that can be utilized in keeping a pulse check on the activities and the resources needed so that a flag can be raised if things start to go sideways.

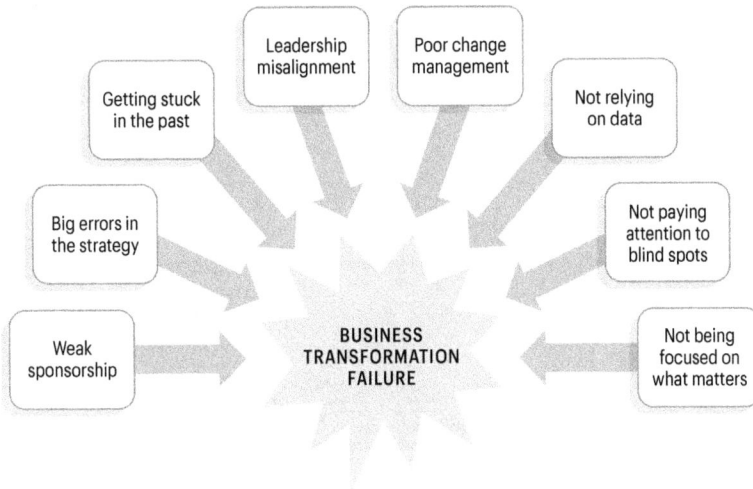

8

How Much Should
We Budget For?

The question that presents itself when businesses initiate organization optimization or transformation activities is: "How much should we spend on this?" The answer, of course, is, "It depends!" And it really does depend—on the circumstances the company is facing, the pace required to change direction or address risk, the magnitude of the transformation, and many other factors.

Typically, organizations do a cost-benefit analysis to outline different options for different transformational engagement. The transformation team outlines for the management what each option would cost, how long it could take, and the potential risks associated with it.

The cost-benefit assessment should clearly articulate what really matters for the organization. Is the company willing to change and transform, is it capable of doing so, and how big should those efforts be? Let me demonstrate by comparing the cost and benefits of buying a Ferrari versus a Toyota. Clearly, a Ferrari will cost much more than a Toyota, but it will likely get you to your destination faster (especially if the journey is short). The Ferrari will be expensive to maintain and repair, but it looks nice and fancy! The Toyota will also take you from point A to point B, but will likely be slower. However, the Toyota is probably more reliable and much cheaper to maintain.

Similarly, a company may be faced with choices that, while not so significantly different, will be hard to choose from. A comprehensive cost-benefit analysis is the best way to illustrate all options and ramifications.

If a team does not have in-house experience creating transformation plans, it is very common to hire consulting agencies that specialize in this field. The team or organization can initiate RFPs from different consulting companies so they can compare what the firms offer, their previous engagements and successes, and the cost associated with the work. The transformation team can create a score card to compare the different proposals and use that to decide which firm to choose as a partner in the transformation journey.

There are many examples of failed transformation activities that were stopped midcourse because the team ran out of money. This can be attributed to factors such as wrong early assumptions or inaccurate data that led to a significant unaffordable change of direction; spending without control especially during planning; not adding a buffer to account for the unexpected; not managing scope creep; or not having a solid and regular tracker.

It is extremely important to include a comprehensive outline of the transformation cost, including those associated with people (insourced and outsourced), technology, process, change management, and data.

Then a solid tracker should be established to ensure that actual spending is being monitored and validated against the budget.

We've now covered the scope of an organization's transformation, and have a better understanding of what a brighter future could look like. Let's consider how to deliver that future through execution and project management.

Why do we keep missing milestones?

Why are our activities not going
as fast as we thought?

Why is our team disjointed and
unable to align on efforts?

Why are we spending more than we budgeted for?

Why can we not see the light
at the end of the tunnel?

Why are the processes so bureaucratic?

Why does the scope keep creeping?

PART TWO

DELIVERY AND PROJECT MANAGEMENT

9

Why Does Delivery Mechanism Matter So Much?

Now that we have considered the reason to change, it is time to focus on the delivery mechanism. The key is to deliver the scope of the strategic initiatives according to a predefined timeline and within an agreed budget. This is what project management is all about. Solid project management discipline is crucial for effective transformation across an organization. According to Project Management Institute (pmi.org), project management is the application of knowledge, skills, tools, and techniques to project activities and meet the project requirements. I will speak in greater detail about the different types of project management practices in the following chapter, but it is important to highlight here the difference between projects, programs, and portfolios. They are all critical components in providing effectiveness and control to optimize the use of resources and funds while ensuring effective governance, stakeholder management, and benefits realization in organizations seeking change and transformation.

A project is a temporary endeavor focused on creating a unique product, service, or result. Project management brings focus and discipline shaped by constraints such as scopes, resources, costs, quality, and the schedule of each project.

A program is a collection of related projects that need to be managed and coordinated to obtain benefits not possible from managing them individually. Program management may involve completing some work that is outside the scope of its individual projects.

A portfolio is a collection of related and unrelated projects and programs that are managed as a group to achieve strategic goals and objectives. Portfolio management balances the prioritization, implementation, and control of change initiatives to deliver the strategic objectives of the organizations.

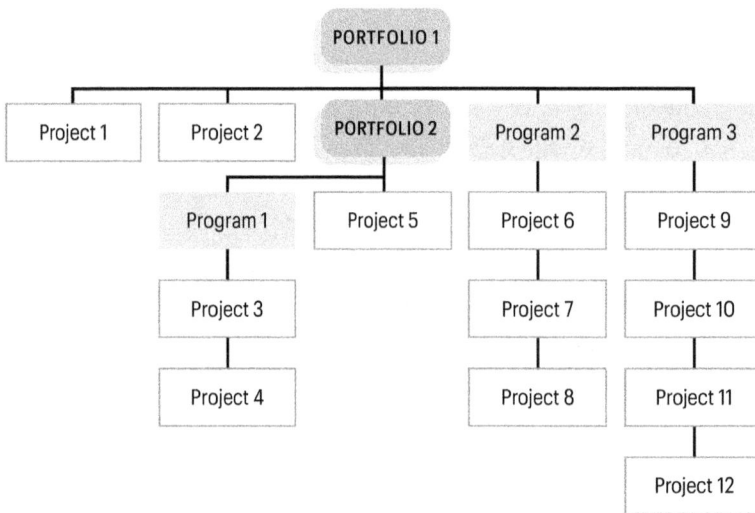

```
                         PORTFOLIO 1
    ┌──────────┬──────────┼──────────┬──────────┐
 Project 1   Project 2  PORTFOLIO 2  Program 2  Program 3
                  ┌──────────┤          │          │
             Program 1   Project 5   Project 6  Project 9
                  │                     │          │
             Project 3              Project 7   Project 10
                  │                     │          │
             Project 4              Project 8   Project 11
                                                   │
                                                Project 12
```

Opportunities almost always exist; there are no excuses not to optimize or transform any company. Organizations that dig and look for opportunities will find them. Opportunities can be outlined in a transformation road map that may include any of the strategies identified in chapter 3 (organic and inorganic strategies).

The problem most companies face is the will of its owners, stock-holders, leaders, and employees. Remember, organizations that do not adapt will eventually die. Winning companies have shareholders, leaders, and employees that are motivated, hungry for opportunities, see the potential, want to grab those opportunities, and have a desire to win and succeed in reaching new heights.

MOVING AT THE SPEED OF CHANGE

Changing to win is nice, but if an organization is slow to figure out the scope and enable that change, it will likely miss the opportunities it has been seeking. Oprah Winfrey once said: "Doing the best at this moment puts you in the best place for the next moment."[7] Many companies have failed to deliver their transformational initiatives because they lack the drive or resources that have an action-oriented mindset. Many organizations linger so long on the objective and analysis that they miss the opportunity presented in the transformation model.

"Changing to win, and fast" should be the focus because competitors (existing and new) are already on a mission to improve their businesses, expand their reach, gain market share, innovate in new products and services, and find ways to win. Also, even with little to no competition, the world is changing, and circumstances may create attrition in the marketplace. Those circumstances can be triggered by weather, government, wars, pandemics, natural resources, or any other factor. Having an action-oriented mindset is one of the most important aspects of delivering solid business transformation. Without this type of enthusiasm and energy, milestones and objectives will be missed. Those organizations that have a good vision and are inspired by action, persistence, and perseverance almost always win.

Whatever the circumstances, there may be options for improvement in the operations or for reduction in waste, but it is important to note that sometimes the best strategy is to be patient and wait for the right timing. Initiate a change that improves the company's products and/or services, paced according to factors surrounding the company. Leaders may decide to delay, pause, or slow down the change for many reasons. Examples include a specific technology being too new and expensive, new trade agreements that may favorably change tariffs, or the economy cycle in recession.

CHANGE TO ADD VALUE

It is crucial to understand the real purpose of an organization's change and avoid superficial improvement that could deplete transformation funds and resources without any meaningful output. The following are examples of values that can be created by transformational projects and how they can be tracked.

Cost saving: This is year-over-year savings that usually can be traced in the general ledger. In other words, the money saved can be counted and recorded in the accounting books. For example, say a company spends $10,000 the previous year on electricity, but with a new project that is implemented to install motion sensors and energy-efficient light bulbs, the electricity bill is reduced to $8,000. In this case, the $2,000 is considered a cost saving. Tracking these savings is fairly easy: review the bills paid and compare year-over-year cost savings.

Cost avoidance: There are times when year-over-year savings are not met by an initiative, but the company still avoids increased costs, and that is definitely a win. For example, suppose a company spends $1 million on building materials one year, but the next year, the vendor decides to increase the price by 5 percent to account for inflation. However, the project team manages to negotiate with the vendor so there is no increase in price. In this case, the team avoids $50,000 extra that they might otherwise have had to pay. Tracking this cost is also not difficult, as the team can review the previous year's cost and document the action they took to avoid the cost increase by the vendor.

Revenue generation: Initiatives can be focused on increasing the company's top line by generating more revenue. This can be accomplished by:

- **Increasing volume from existing customers:** Increasing promotions and marketing efforts to trigger more purchases while maintaining customer satisfaction or finding new use of a company's products or services would allow existing customers to buy more of those products or services. For example, marketing the durability of the paper towels a company produces may allow customers to use them not only in the kitchen but also in the garage, office, and bathrooms. This increase of value can be tracked by comparing the units sold period over period.

- **Increasing market share:** Attracting new customers who will purchase a new or existing product or service offered by the organization is not easy but can be achieved by increasing awareness and marketing efforts. For example, a superior camera resolution may not only keep existing cell phone customers from switching to a new phone brand, but also convince customers who are using an inferior product to acquire the new product. The company can track the number of customers by establishing a loyalty program and create a database that tracks the number of customers and their purchases.

- **Increasing prices:** An organization may increase the prices of its products or services when it is safe to do so without causing the customers to abandon those products or services. An initiative to increase prices may be driven by new features or faster services based on customer demand and competition dynamics. If competition raises prices and the organization's product is similar, the organization can also potentially raise prices to match or be only slightly less than the competitors'. Tracking is achieved by closely monitoring markets and using advanced analytics.

- **Increasing a company's value:** Company leaders may focus their initiatives on increasing the value of their organization. This is usually driven by increased revenue, increased profit margin, increased cash flow, or increased market share. However, the company's strategy may focus on increasing its assets through innovation. For example, a company may be focusing its initiatives on securing as many patents as it can in order to one day capitalize on those innovations; this is not uncommon in the pharmaceutical and tech industries.

Soft benefits: An organization may focus on other important aspects such as customer and employee satisfaction, code green pioneering, or just the company's image. These are all extremely important elements that sustain the organization's operations and drive growth. The soft benefits will directly or indirectly lead to hard benefits such as revenue generation and cost savings/avoidance. Measuring the soft benefits can be achieved by means of KPIs and surveys that measure any shift in those attributes.

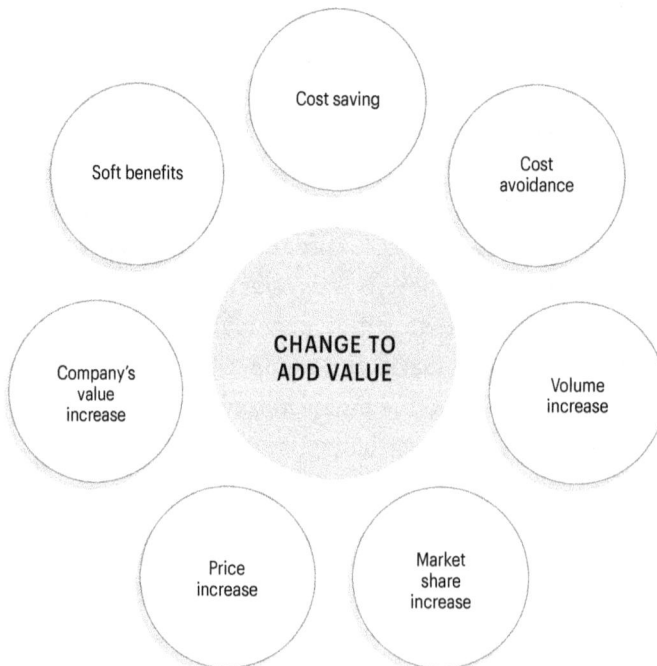

Sometimes, driving execution too fast can cause fatal errors that arise as a result of not paying attention to team alignment, missing critical communication, increasing bureaucracy, and overstretching resources. Change management is a particularly important topic that is easily missed and will be highlighted in Part Three of this book.

Strong leadership and motivated team members should be assigned to lead the delivery efforts toward change. What delivery mechanism to choose, how to drive execution, where to start from, who is engaged in the activities, and how the budgeted funds have been managed all matter greatly.

PRIORITIZATION OF EFFORTS

Organizations may want to prioritize objectives and rank them as follows:

- **Must have:** Those objectives that are fundamental to achieving a defined future state. In other words, unless those goals are reached, there will be no value captured.

- **Should have:** These are important elements that will enable an optimal future state. Without these elements, the company will operate inefficiently; the destination will be reached, but processes or technologies may be suboptimal.

- **Nice to have:** These are items that will be useful and could add value but are secondary in terms of priority. Tangible benefits may be utilized by addressing these items, but the efforts may not be worthwhile unless all must-have and should-have objectives have first been met.

BUREAUCRACY VERSUS GOVERNANCE

Efficiency and simplicity are needed at all levels of change, as complexity can add layers of confusion, disconnection, and misalignment among team members and stakeholders.

Avoid bureaucracy, especially in large organizations that have matrix structures with many departments and locations. Complicated processes and roadblocks create confusion and frustration in the organization. Plus, people tend to try find alternatives and figure out how to do the job themselves, which could create shadow organizations that do not align with the overall direction of the enterprise.

Also, bureaucracy slows down any efforts toward "speed to market"—in other words, launching and deploying new products and services to customers before competitors.

Governance is different and encouraged to ensure efficiency while focusing on what matters. Without governance, an organization will suffer from lack of alignment, missed opportunities to scale efforts, and poor deployment of funds and resources, which could derail any transformational effort.

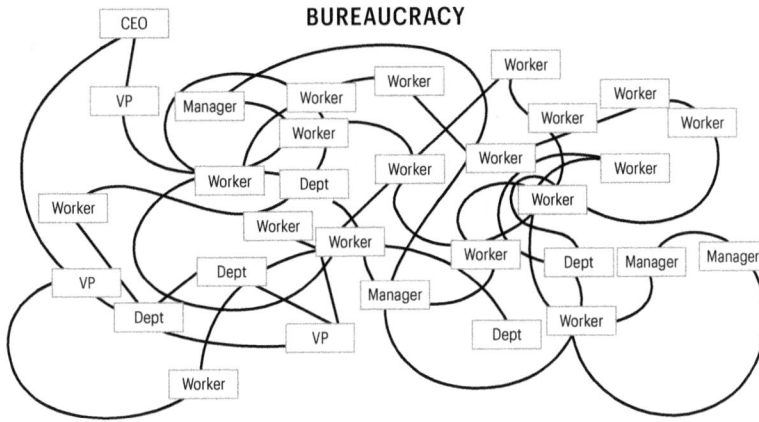

BUREAUCRACY

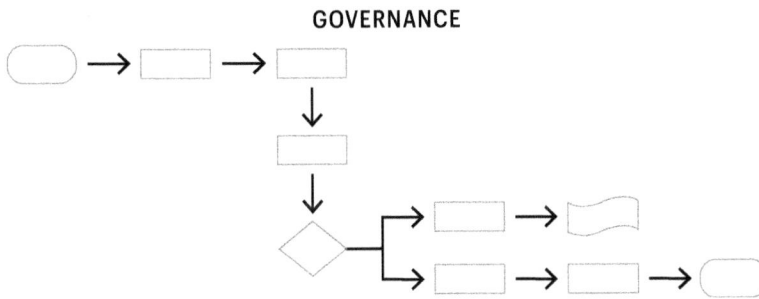

GOVERNANCE

10

What Tools and Techniques Should We Use?

Any transformation effort or change initiative is basically a project. Many people do not understand the difference between operations and projects. They tend to think that managing projects is part of their day job, and while that can be true for those who are project managers, it is mostly an inaccurate assumption made by the majority of a company's employees. Therefore, it will be helpful to remember the definition of a project.

Project: A temporary endeavor undertaken to create a unique product, service, or result. The two important elements here are:

1. Temporary: It has a defined beginning and end, a defined scope, and defined resources.

2. Unique: It is not a routine operation but a specific set of tasks designed to accomplish a unique goal.

The following are examples of projects from a few industries:

- In the design and construction industries, a project will eventually design and build something that did not exist before; or, it may demolish or renovate something that existed in the past.

- In the IT industry, a project will create, develop, or improve something that is technology-related, such as software, infrastructure, systems, technical solutions, cybersecurity protocol, and data integration.

- In the service industry, most services are repetitive in nature and follow the operation definition, such as a call center agent answering and accommodating customer needs, a cashier collecting money, and so on. However, a project can create a new standard operating procedure (SOP) and either improve the service (such as increased turnaround time) or add certain value (such as offering more products or services to the customers).

- In the manufacturing industry, while a production line may be creating a product (cars, phones, pens, etc.), this is typically an operation that is repetitive. A project can be launched to add a feature to a product by changing elements in the production line to enhance operations or add or remove certain components.

There are endless examples of projects and many can be cross-industry and cross-functional, which means those projects can do more than one thing at time and will utilize combined efforts from different industries or different functions. For example, an IT team may help a call center department implement a new system, software, or hardware to improve their capabilities and serve the customer faster and better.

In the spirit of optimization and transformation projects, the nature of these initiatives is usually improvement-focused. Improvement-focused projects have a defined scope to change certain operations and add value, and then create new procedures that usually become part of the new operation.

Here is an example that illustrates this flow:

- Existing operation: The front desk staff of a hotel have daily recurring and repetitive "operating" work: to welcome hotel guests, validate their IDs, ensure room selection is still valid for the guests, give them their room keys, and ensure that their needs are met.

- Improvement project: The need for change is identified. A project is launched to speed up the check-in process (higher customer satisfaction) and promote suites that have a higher price tag (increase profit). A special team of five cross-functional people is created to kick off this unique initiative with a plan to finalize it in three months. The project team manages to create new SOPs and train front desk staff as well as provide them with the tools for success.

- New operation: The front desk staff now has new operating procedures that they follow on a daily basis. The project team adjourn and potentially start tackling other projects.

Now that we understand what a project is, it is time to pick which method of project management is needed for different initiatives within the transformational effort of a company. There are several project management practices. Some may be applicable to certain initiatives at a specific time, while others may not be very effective for those types of projects. It's all in making the right choice of practice for the job and then following the applicable best practices related to the selected method. As Michael Jordan said, "You can practice shooting eight hours a day, but if your technique is wrong, then all you become is very good at shooting the wrong way."[8]

PROJECT MANAGEMENT PRACTICES

There are several project management methodologies, and some are more popular in certain practices and industries than others. It is important to note that more than one practice can be used for a project, but care should be applied in order to avoid confusion and the collision of mandates from different methodologies among the project team.

The following are the most popular project management methodologies:

Waterfall/Traditional

This is the most widely used project management method. In essence, the Waterfall relies on a linear approach, where each stage of a project is completed before another begins. The project team starts with defining the scope and requirements for the project, and estimates a budget to be allocated to that project. After the scope and budget are approved by the senior leaders, the project team puts a plan in place to guide them on how to deliver the requirements. The team will also assign resources to every task in the project plan and put a tracker to monitor spending. They will go through the design, build, test, and deploy phases in a sequential pattern throughout the project before they deliver the final scope and close it accordingly.

The name "Waterfall" comes from the sequential nature of this method, as everything should flow one way in a linear pattern, like a waterfall, typically shown in a Gantt Chart (a visual project plan). This method initially started, and is still widely used, in the construction and manufacturing industries because usually the end state is clear. For example, a building's (or product's) location, shape, height, design, function, finish, and so on can be determined on the drawing boards and in the requirement documents. Then the team will build accordingly. One of the drawbacks of this method is the lack of flexibility when the designs or specifications change midway.

Usually, the project plan is outlined and dependencies are figured out; then, a critical path is determined to ensure interdependent activities are managed well. The critical path outlines the critical and noncritical activities needed for the project. The critical path is the longest sequence of activities in a project plan, which must be completed on time for the project to be completed on the due date.

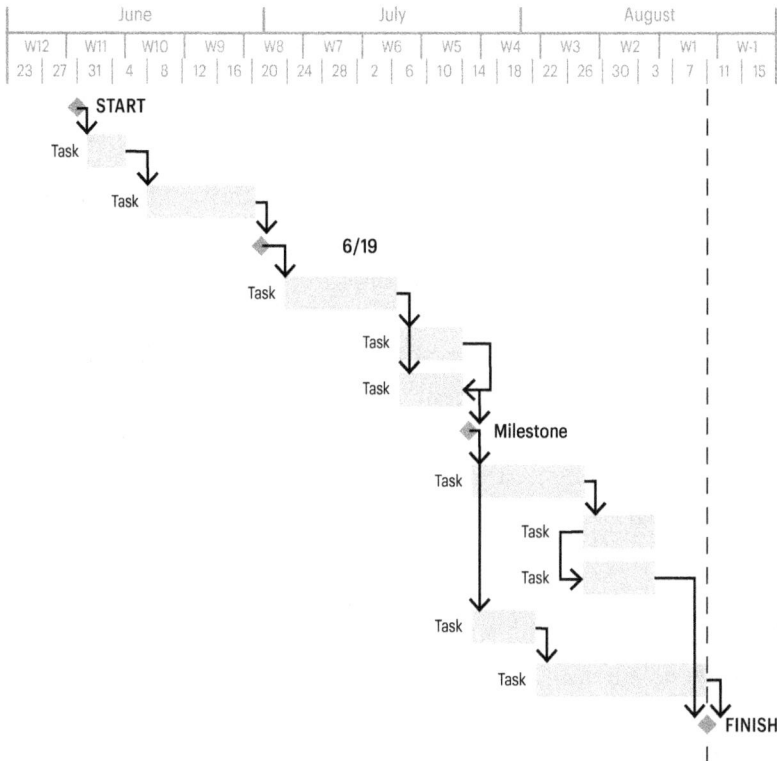

June				July				August			
W12	W11	W10	W9	W8	W7	W6	W5	W4	W3	W2	W1	W-1
23	27	31	4	8	12	16	20	24	28	2	6	10	14	18	22	26	30	3	7	11	15

START

Task

Task

6/19

Task

Task

Task

Milestone

Task

Task

Task

Task

Task

FINISH

An activity on the critical path cannot be started until its predecessor activity is complete. If an activity on the critical path is delayed, the entire project will be delayed, unless the activity following the delay is completed earlier than originally planned.

For example, if the scope is to build a house, the team cannot install electrical outlets before the walls are installed; the walls cannot be installed until the concrete foundation is poured and sets; the concrete cannot be poured until the foundation has been dug and cement truck arrives at the site; the foundation cannot be dug until a design and permits are complete, and the cement quantity has been calculated and ordered and so on! Those interdependent tasks are all on the critical path, and if any one of them is delayed, it stands to reason that the whole project will be delayed. One project management best practice is to add a buffer or "float" (also called "slack") in the project plan to account for any unplanned delays. By definition, float/slack means the amount of time that a task can be delayed without causing a delay to the entire project.

If a project faces delays and project leaders want to catch up, then there are two main ways to resolve that issue when activities are not on the critical path and can be overlapped:

- **Fast tracking:** The team can perform activities in tandem to compress the schedule. For example, part of the team can install roof shingles while other team members complete the heating and air-conditioning installation. One potential drawback is that this approach can cause increases in rework and risk.

- **Crashing:** Basically, the team can add resources to the activities to compress the schedule. For example, instead of having two painters to complete the house painting, the project manager can hire six and finish the work sooner. The drawback of this approach is the increased labor cost, and risk, too.

The Waterfall approach can be very powerful in projects that require solid control to deliver a defined end state according to deadline and within budget. This method has faced challenges in areas such as product and software development, mainly due to a lack of adaptability to change designs frequently and collect and incorporate customer feedback during the process.

The Project Management Institute (PMI) has been setting standards for project management practices for years. The PMI came up with a Project Management Body of Knowledge (PMBOK) to outline a set of standards, terminologies, and guidelines in the industry. The standards in the PMBOK align well with the Waterfall methodology and provide excellent references and best practices to position these types of projects for success.

Fundamentally, the PMBOK outlines five process groups (basically phases), and ten knowledge areas that are prevalent in most, if not every, project.

Process Groups

Initiating: In this phase, the team tries to define and get an approval on the scope of the project, find sources of funds, identify key stakeholders, and get official approval to kick off the project.

Planning: In this step, the scope gets refined and the tasks are outlined throughout the project with clear milestones to hit along the journey. Documents are produced to clarify specifications, designs, testing criteria, plans for resources, roles and responsibilities, communications, fund disbursement and tracking, decision matrix, and risk assessments.

Executing: This phase simply means executing the work and delivering according to the project plan.

Monitoring and controlling: This is a phase that goes from the beginning of the project until the end. The purpose of this monitoring and controlling is to do pulse checks along the way to ensure the project is progressing as planned and that impediments are removed. Key deliverables in this phase are status reports, performance tracking, budget tracking, quality control, issues and risk reviews, actions to address, and decisions to be logged.

Closing: This is the conclusion of the activities in any given project. There are a few steps in this phase related to cleaning up any sites, releasing resources, training operators or customers, organizing documentation, celebrating success, reconciling budget, and documenting lessons learned.

These phases are not meant to be completely sequential. Initiation activities might happen at the same time as planning work, for example. Execution and planning usually go through several cycles, but at a certain time, planning is reduced and execution activities peak. Finally, as the project reaches the closing phase, the closing activities start to peak while all planning or execution activities end because the work is done. Monitoring and controlling starts from the early stages and continues to the very last stage of the project, and those activities usually peak during the heaving planning and execution. The following diagram helps explain visually the level of efforts applied during each phase of the project.

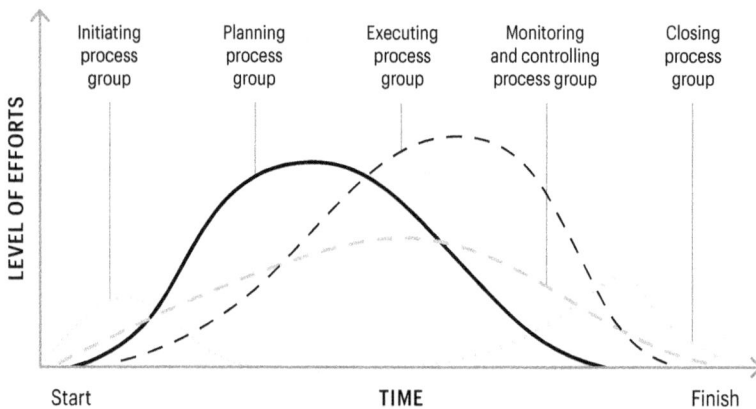

Knowledge Areas

Based on the PMBOK, successful project leaders have to be experienced in the following knowledge areas.

Integration management: The leaders must ensure that all elements and dependencies in the project and other projects that could impact or be impacted are identified and coordinated. Most projects and elements within each project do not exist in a silo, so coordination is vital to ensure alignment and remove ambiguities.

Scope management: It is vital that the leaders understand the requirements of every project, and what is in scope versus out of scope. Many projects fail to meet their objectives simply because the original goals are expanded while they are in progress. Scope creep can be a result of poor control, lack of proper scoping and clear objectives, weak project leaders and sponsors who say yes to every demand without realizing ramifications, and, of course, poor communication between stakeholders.

Schedule/time management: The project team should be able to draft clear project plans and understand dependencies. They also need to account for holidays, special events, vacations, and seasonal and regional events, and ensure that the plans are realistic and achievable without relaxing the timeline too much and jeopardizing the benefits of the project.

Cost management: No project is delivered without being funded. People, supplies, equipment, fuel, and many other inputs cost money. The project leaders should be able to estimate the budget needed to kick off and complete the project according to scope and timelines. Also, proper approvals should be obtained before the project starts. Adding a certain amount of money in the budget as a contingency is very highly recommended to account for unexpected events or expenses. Tracking the spending and reporting to the project sponsors are very important, to ensure the project does not run out of money along the way.

Quality management: This can be broken down into determining the expected quality standards of the deliverable and ensuring quality control and an efficient process in reaching the goals. Establishing expectations of quality is important for customer satisfaction, but the quality standards have a major impact on the project cost and timeline. The higher the quality needed, the longer and more expensive it usually is for the project team to complete the desired products or services. The second element related to quality management is ensuring quality control and assurance along the way, which helps guarantee that the expected product or service is delivered and that the work to accomplish that objective meets quality standards related to set criteria for efficiency and productivity.

Human resource management: Planning for resources is a fundamental part of every project. It involves asking some of the following questions: When do people need to engage? What skillsets are required? Are people expected to be full time or part time? Does the company have the needed resources, and does it have them ready by the time they are needed? Finally, should the project team rely on contracted and outsourced labor? Capacity management plays a key role in determining the human resources needed throughout the project.

Communication management: Communication is one of the most important elements in any project. It refers to not only what is being communicated, but also how it is communicated. Communication management includes the type, senders, receivers, timing, external/internal, and frequency of communication needed during the project. Examples of questions to be answered regarding communication planning are: How will statuses, risks, issues, and progress be delivered to different stakeholders? Will the communication be through email, bulletin board, town halls, in person, or another way? What will the message be and how can it be made effective for the specific audience without creating confusion and anxiety? Does the person delivering the message have the right influence, characteristics, authority, and skills to make it impactful and effective?

Risk management: Risk management will be highlighted in detail in Part Four of this book; those techniques to identify and address risk apply to any project and should be part of a risk management plan.

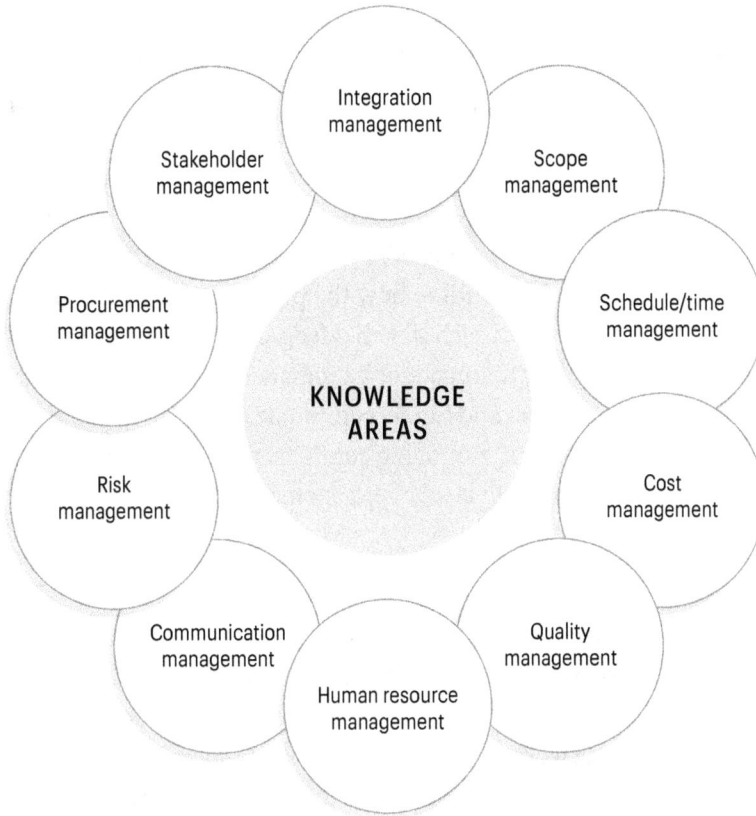

Procurement management: Product, information, and/or services may need to be acquired during the project's life cycle. Procurement management outlines the items needed to be purchased or leased, the availability of those items, the turnaround time for them to arrive, their sources, and prices. Activities may involve vendors and include requests for information (RFIs), RFPs, or RFQs.

Purchasing activities may or may not be complicated depending on the scope of the project. Purchase approval flow and authority for dollar threshold should be established in the beginning of the project to ensure proper control and to avoid depletion of the budget and any unauthorized spending. In some organizations, legal or other mandatory approvals need to be obtained prior to making certain purchases. Planning, conducting, administering, and closing purchases are all part of good procurement management practice within a project.

Stakeholder management: Stakeholders are those who will be affected by the project at any point during its life cycle. Stakeholders can be individuals, organizations, and communities. Stakeholder management activities outline how the project and its team members should interact with each stakeholder group based on their level or interest and ability to impact or be impacted by the project. Part of this activity is proper and timely communication plans, managing needs and expectations, removing conflicts, eliminating ambiguity, and allowing for the right level of engagement as needed.

Agile

The Agile method is often used when a project's end state is not clearly defined or there is a high degree of uncertainty and complexity. This approach relies on iterative and incremental deliverables, where the project team presents a version of the solution every cycle, shares progress and prototypes with a group of customers or users, receives feedback on what needs to change, and then makes modifications and improvements to best fit their needs. The team repeats the same iterative cycle to make suggested changes and improvements while presenting to the customers or users to get feedback until the solution meets most, if not all, of the requirements, and it is ready to be launched.

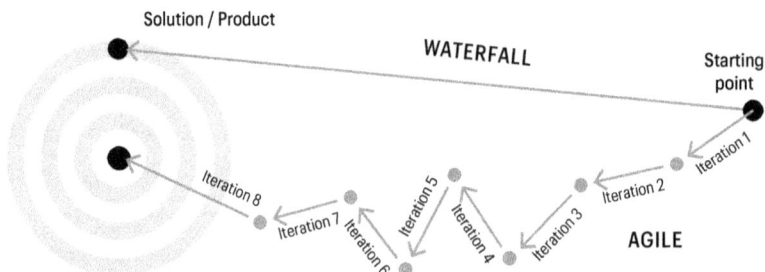

Agile fits the types of projects that require flexibility and speed, such as the development of software, websites, and products. The project team can usually adjust things rapidly as mandates change and incorporate feedback in the solutions they are developing. The Agile method was initially established for software development projects because Waterfall was too rigid and could not handle the continual, rapid changes in the requirements of such projects. Through Agile, the project team can increase their ability to manage changing priorities, provide visibility of the solution at hand, align between different functions, and deliver the solution to the market faster.

A group of software industry leaders created the Agile Manifesto (agilemanifesto.org) in 2001 and provided some outlines on how the practice can work to enable iterative development, team collaboration, and change recognition while reducing paperwork and documentation.

The following are the four Agile Values outlined in the Manifesto:

1   Individuals and interactions over processes and tools
2   Working software over comprehensive documentation
3   Customer collaboration over contract negotiation
4   Responding to change over following a plan

The Manifesto also highlighted its Twelve Principles:

1   Customer satisfaction through early and continuous software delivery
2   Accommodate changing requirements throughout the development process
3   Frequent delivery of working software
4   Collaboration between the business stakeholders and developers throughout the project
5   Support, trust, and motivate the people involved
6   Enable face-to-face interactions
7   Working software is the primary measure of progress
8   Agile processes to support a consistent development pace

9 Attention to technical detail and design enhances agility

10 Simplicity

11 Self-organizing teams encourage great architectures, requirements, and designs

12 Regular reflections on how to become more effective[9]

Agile is not just a set of practices and tools; it is a mindset to enable
iterative delivery of solutions that meet or exceed customer needs.
The team can tailor their Agile methodology to their own circumstances to adapt to certain environments and needs.

In a typical Agile practice, the team works initially on a product from
a solution vision statement and outlines a road map. Then, they create a backlog and release plan. The next step is for the team to go
through multiple sprints or iterations while holding retrospective
meetings to collect feedback from the team or customers.

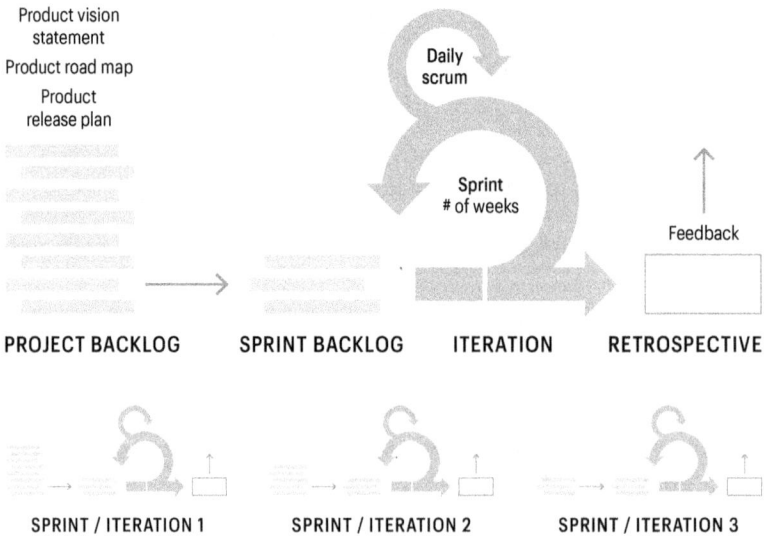

Product vision
statement

Product road map

Product
release plan

Daily
scrum

Sprint
# of weeks

Feedback

PROJECT BACKLOG   **SPRINT BACKLOG**   **ITERATION**   **RETROSPECTIVE**

SPRINT / ITERATION 1   **SPRINT / ITERATION 2**   **SPRINT / ITERATION 3**

Agile is a methodology that has practices within itself—such as scrum, Extreme Programming (XP), the Dynamic Systems Development Method (DSDM), Feature-Driven Development (FDD), Crystal—and others, such as Lean Product Development (LPD) and Kanban. The following sections will shed light on some of the most common Agile derivatives.

Scrum: Scrum is the most popular Agile practice and is based on three pillars:

1. Transparency: The most important part of the scrum method is to give people responsible for outcomes full visibility into the process and the current state of the product/solution. The frequent reviews give stakeholders and customers a clear view into the status of the solution.

2. Inspection: This provides a proactive process to prevent defects in the solution. The team, stakeholders, and/or customers inspect the solution or product at regular intervals along the way during the sprint reviews and retrospectives.

3. Adaptation: If an inspection shows any issues, then the team adapts and adjusts the process and the solution or product as soon as possible.

Scrum features various "sessions," sometimes defined as "sprints," which generally last fifteen or thirty days. These sprints are used to prioritize various project tasks and ensure they are completed within this time.

Rather than being a project manager, a scrum master should facilitate the process and assemble small teams that have oversight of specific tasks.

Scrum's ultimate goal is to design, develop, deliver, and sustain complex solutions or products through collaboration, accountability, and an iterative process. To enable this, the scrum practice establishes clear events to complete and roles to be assumed along the process.

Scrum events

- Sprint: A time box where iterative goals are delivered. Usually the time frame varies between one and four weeks and is consistent throughout the project's life cycle.

- Sprint planning: The scrum team meeting at the beginning of every sprint to plan the upcoming sprint.

- Daily scrum: Typically, a ten-to-fifteen-minute meeting held every day of the sprint at the same time. It is also called a "daily standup," and the objective is to ask each member three questions to be answered in thirty to sixty seconds: What were the accomplishments of the prior day? What are the objectives today? What are the impediments faced?

- Sprint review or retrospective: A meeting held at the end of every sprint for the scrum team to present the increment deliverable to the stakeholders or customers, collect feedback, discuss the feedback, and document changes to be addressed in the next sprint.

Scrum team roles

- Product owner: A person who is "the voice of the customer." That person should be knowledgeable about the solution or product features and specifications the customers are seeking, and empowered to make decisions on behalf of those customers.

- Development team: This team has a number of professionals who are able to deliver the solution or product in scope. The team usually contains designers, developers, programmers, and engineers.

- Scrum master: A facilitator who is well organized and has leadership traits to influence the team, bring alignment, help prioritize backlogs, and ensure proper execution of scrums toward a solution that meets or exceeds customer needs.

Extreme Programming (XP): This is an Agile method that is focused on software development and that advocates for simplicity, communication, feedback, courage, and respect.

Feature-Driven Development (FDD): This Agile approach focuses on the product and builds a feature list to move through design and building in an interactive manner.

Dynamic Systems Development Method (DSDM): This is one of the earlier Agile methods that covers a project's life cycle from feasibility to implementation.

Crystal: This is a combination of methods that can be customized by criticality and size, usually indicated by color, from Crystal Clear (low-important project built by small team) all the way on the spectrum to Crystal Magenta (critical project built by a large team).

Lean and Six Sigma

Lean practice aims to reduce or eliminate waste. Six Sigma focuses on reducing variations or defects and works on achieving consistent results. The Lean practice took shape between the 1920s and 1950s when statisticians and quality-control pioneers Walter Shewhart and W. Edwards Deming emphasized the observation of operations and created the Plan-Do-Check-Act cycle to help organizations achieve process improvement.

The Lean and Six Sigma practice was introduced in the 1950s by the Japanese Toyota Production System (TPS), which revolutionized the manufacturing process. The name Six Sigma comes from the standard deviations, or sigma, represented by the Greek letter "σ", between the mean and nearest specification limit. The Six Sigma goal is to reach 99.99966 percent yield and achieve no more than 3.4 defects per million units produced.

The following table highlights the differences in expected defect outputs between 1 and 6 Sigma:

SIGMA	YIELD	DEFECTS PER MILLION
6	99.99966%	3.4
5	99.977%	230
4	99.379%	6,210
3	93.32%	66,800
2	69.2%	308,000
1	31%	690,000

Six Sigma relies heavily on data and uses statistical and empirical quality techniques to identify variations in the process to reduce or eliminate defects. Lean Six Sigma utilizes the Six Sigma tools and techniques to reduce or eliminate waste. When done properly, those practices can increase quality, lower costs, and improve processes. General Electric was one of the companies that pioneered Six Sigma in the 1990s and claimed to realize billions of dollars of benefits.

While Lean and Six Sigma began in manufacturing, they have been also used by thousands of companies in other industries, including the service sector and software development. As mentioned earlier, one Agile methodology is LPD, and it focuses primarily on eliminating waste during the product development cycle.

One of Six Sigma's core tactics, Belts, adapted from martial arts, is used to create multilevel expertise within organizations. The Belts hierarchy helps cascade and spread the Six Sigma practice across different levels within organizations and tackle opportunities wherever they exist. The following illustrates the different Belt levels and objectives, in descending order:

- Master Black Belt: A seasoned Black Belt who can certify, train, and mentor other Belts.

- Black Belt: Fully trained and dedicated to reducing waste or improving processes and quality.

- Green Belt: Understands and knows how to use some tools and does so while performing their day job.

- Yellow Belt: Aware of the methods and some basic techniques and can use them on the job.

- White Belt: Basic knowledge of the techniques and tools available and usually unable to use them.

The major methodologies utilized in Lean and Six Sigma are:

DMAIC: Used for improving current business processes, solutions, products, or services.

- **D:** Define the problem
- **M:** Measure the various aspects of the current state
- **A:** Analyze data to find errors/waste and figure out solutions
- **I:** Improve the process, solution, product, or service
- **C:** Control to measure and ensure that the new solution continues to work

DMADV: Used to completely redesign or create new processes, solutions, products, or services. DMADV is also similar to DFSS (Design for Six Sigma).

- **D:** Define the goal
- **M:** Measure components and capabilities
- **A:** Analyze data to develop and pick a design/solution
- **D:** Design and test the solution
- **V:** Verify that the designed solution works, simulate, pilot, deploy, and collect feedback

OPDCA: Used often in Lean and is a repeatable process.

- **O:** Observe the situation
- **P:** Plan a solution
- **D:** Do what is needed to resolve the issue
- **C:** Check if the solution is working
- **A:** Act (also Adjust) to refine the solution if needed

The Lean mindset focuses on reducing waste and identifies three types of deviations, called 3Ms, adopted from the Japanese terms Muda, Mura, and Muri.

Muda (waste): Activities or processes that create waste and do not add value. The eight main types of waste can be summarized as follows (TIM WOODS):

1. Transport: Excess product movement between locations or operation units causes waste in fuel, energy, and time, as well as asset depreciation.

2. Inventory: Any excess inventory is a waste of space and capital, whether it is finished goods or work in progress (WIP).

3. Motion: Unnecessary physical movement of a person or machine during any operation or activity wastes time and energy, and is potentially lost opportunity.

4. Wait: Waiting for a service or product or a process to finish or arrive is a waste of time and resources.

5. Overproduction: Overproducing a product or output beyond what customers need wastes materials, resources, energy, and potentially storage cost. If the product is perishable, the money spent on over-produced product is wasted.

6. Overprocessing: Overdoing any activity, service, or operation beyond what is needed also wastes time, resources, and energy. It may also add frustration instead of helping deliver objectives.

7. Defects: If a defect in a product or service is discovered before it is delivered to customers, the waste is in disposal and rework. If the product or service is delivered to the customer, the waste and cost could be multifold. In addition to the rework and disposal of defected items, the consequences could be shipping and handling costs, loss of customers, loss of opportunity, loss of trust in the product or service, media costs spent to try and rectify the situation, legal fees, and potential compensation for causing any harm due to that defect.

8. Skills: Nonutilized resources are a big source of waste in organizations: employees may be better utilized in different roles, functions, or locations. This particular waste is very hard to quantify, but it can be quite costly to organizations.

Mura (unevenness): Fluctuation in process, product, or service output can cause frustration and a loss of opportunity. Moreover, variation may also introduce other deviations such as Muda (waste) and Muri (overburden). Fluctuation may cause customer rejection and therefore wasted effort, time, and materials. It also may require fast rework to satisfy customers, which may overload resources or machines. For example, if a restaurant chain produces different sizes of burgers and different types of ingredients instead of consistently offering the same expected quality, size, and ingredients to customers, those customers may not be satisfied with the burger they get and may reject it. That can cause not only customer dissatisfaction and frustration but also a waste of materials, as well as overload resources and machines to reproduce a burger that customers expect.

Muri (overburden): Overloading resources and machines may cause employee turnover, safety concerns, machine breakdowns, and potential slowdown of processes. This can be attributed to things such as lack of clarity regarding priorities, poor leadership, using incorrect tools, suboptimal time management, and poor organization skills. Sometimes, when the process is too lean, Muda (waste) can cause Muri (overburden) because people and machines are working at or more than 100 percent, which can result in Mura (unevenness) because of fatigue. Preventive tactics such as performing regular maintenance on machines and offering breaks to employees reduces Muri.

Kanban

Kanban is often used in Lean and Agile methods. It provides a visual representation of what needs to be done, what is currently in progress, and what is being completed, using a whiteboard and notes. In earlier days (though they are sometimes still used), sticky notes were used, with each note containing the description of a task. Those sticky notes were placed on the whiteboard under several columns, showing the sequence of tasks from To Do, Doing, and Done. The Doing column can be broken down into several more columns showing different sequential workflow efforts that lead to Done. When a team is able to move a task from one stage to the next, this is reflected on the whiteboard, such that the task's sticky note is moved from one column to the next in line, until all of the notes reach the Done stage. In this way, teams can easily see what tasks are coming up, which ones are being worked on, where each task is located along the journey, and which are finished. Usually, different colors of notes can be used to illustrate different work packages, and sometimes they can be grouped together in each column to differentiate those tasks from the rest. Many times, "swim lanes" are used to show different prioritization or categorization within each column. If a new task is added, the team can easily see it in the To Do column; then, those items in that column are prioritized by the team so that those with the highest priorities are moved down the road first until they reach Done.

Kanban has gained popularity in recent years because it provides the following benefits:

- Flexibility
- Visualization
- Prioritization
- Limitation of WIP
- Workflow management
- Collaboration and communication
- Evolution

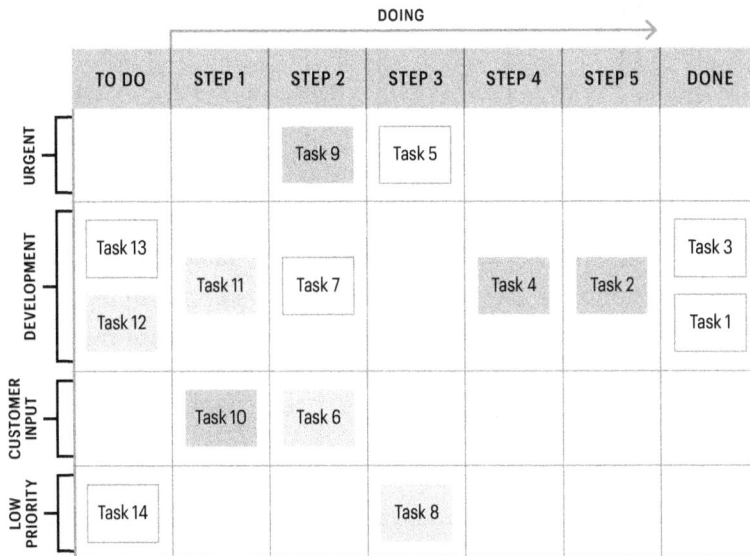

	TO DO	STEP 1	STEP 2	STEP 3	STEP 4	STEP 5	DONE
URGENT			Task 9	Task 5			
DEVELOPMENT	Task 13	Task 11	Task 7		Task 4	Task 2	Task 3
	Task 12						Task 1
CUSTOMER INPUT		Task 10	Task 6				
LOW PRIORITY	Task 14			Task 8			

DOING

Kanban is best suited to projects whose workflow plan includes room to adapt and deliver results in increments, such as in product or software development. Nowadays, there are many online software programs that allow several teams across the world to work on a digital Kanban board and collaborate in real time to update and move the cards virtually from one step to another.

Other Project Management Methods

Stage Gate (Phase Gate): A method used often in new product design and deployment. Similar to Agile, the Stage Gate practice is an iterative approach utilized to promote frequent delivery, customer input, and regular reflection to ensure products meet or exceed the expectations of customers. This method usually uses multiple phases to scope, create, develop, test, and deploy a product. Between each stage is a gate to do quality control and assess the products, cost, and changing scope.

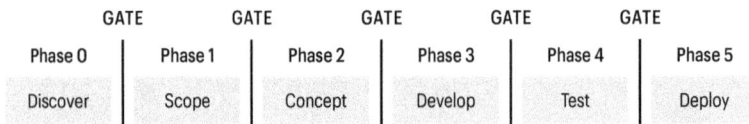

	GATE		GATE		GATE		GATE		GATE	
Phase 0		Phase 1		Phase 2		Phase 3		Phase 4		Phase 5
Discover		Scope		Concept		Develop		Test		Deploy

SDLC: This process method was created to help develop, change, maintain, and replace software systems. The name stands for Software Development Life Cycle. The process starts with input and defined goals from all stakeholders (customers, team members, salespeople, experts). Then, the team starts defining requirements, outlining specifications, and putting together a plan.

The next step is to design according to the specifications outlined in the previous step. The team can now begin to develop and build the software, to be followed by testing for defects and deficiencies, with effort applied to fix all errors until the software meets specifications.

Once that is accomplished, the team works on deployment to allow users and customers to start using what they built. The software may require fixes when first deployed, since sometimes the actual use flags issues that were never thought of during the design and testing.

Finally, the team works on maintaining the software and ensuring that it continuously fits the needs. Frequent version updates are typical to ensure the software continues to work as required. When changes are bigger than simple upgrades or updates, the team may go through two types of further changes:

1. Refactoring: Relatively small changes to the software in order to enhance the capabilities and usage. Usually, the external behavior of the software does not change, but the internal structure and architecture are improved.

2. Reengineering: Major changes to the entire software program. The way the software works is altered by fundamentally changing the codes and drastically redesigning and rebuilding the software.

DevOps: This method was created to break down the barrier between Dev (Development) and Ops (Operations). Its purpose is also similar to Agile in many ways, such as increasing collaboration, sharing responsibilities, and allowing for full transparency. The DevOps team aims to resolve issues faster and minimize operation downtime. The method itself also introduces automation and standardized tools and processes to allow for faster solutions in general, increased productivity, and quicker solutions for unplanned work or bugs.

PRINCE2 (PRojects IN Controlled Environments): This process-based method is popular in the United Kingdom, and it is applied in technology environments. One of the main objectives of this practice is to focus on controls and ensure that they are in place before work is even begun on a project. These control processes cover all the activities throughout the project, from start to finish.

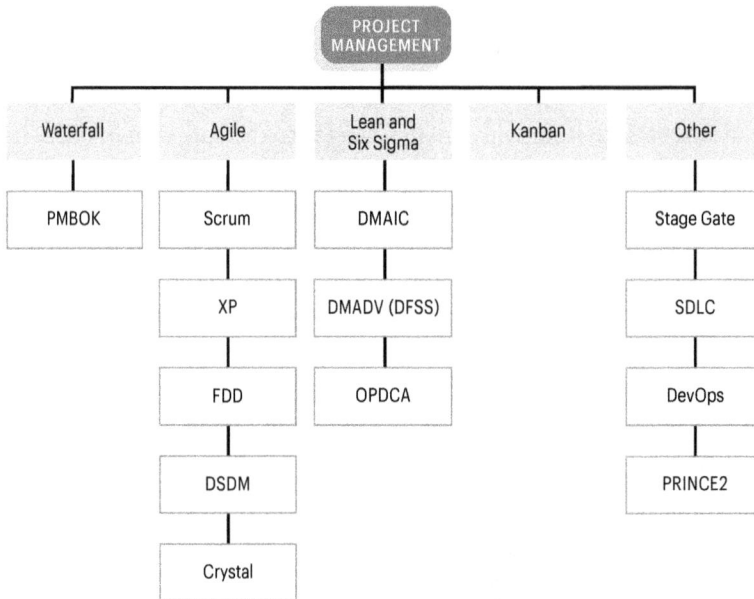

So, which project management method should you choose? While this chapter shed light on a few popular project management methodologies, there are many other approaches to project management that are being used and utilized.

Since businesses and projects vary according to industry, type, size, impact, and many other factors, there is no one project management method that fits all of them. Project leaders should be knowledgeable and familiar with different methods to deliver projects, because one or more of these methods can apply to one or more projects within an organization. It all depends on the project.

There are advantages and disadvantages to every project management methodology. Many organizations use the Waterfall approach, and it has proved effective in many cases, especially for projects with a defined end state. However, when the end state is unclear and there is a need for an evolving approach, Agile and Stage Gate can be utilized—but those also have issues, such as lack of control over budget and frequent schedule slippage.

If used well, a hybrid approach can be very effective, using the best elements from more than one method. For example, the overall program can be run in Waterfall and utilize certain artifacts to control schedule and budget, while some projects or components within the program, such as product, software, or solution development, can be run in Agile.

The following are some of the criteria that can help determine which project management method to apply for a certain project at a certain time in a certain organization:

- Company culture
- Type of leaders
- Organizational goals
- Desired outcome or scope
- Goal criteria (unclear, clear, changing, fixed)
- Project size
- Project budget
- Project timeline
- Project constraints
- Technical background of stakeholders
- Risk tolerance of leaders and team members

In the current business environment, speed and simplicity are crucial. Business and project leaders need to be nimble, keep things simple, inspire their teams, promote communication and feedback, and efficiently deliver objectives.

11

Where Should We Start?

Everything starts with data. Data offers opportunities to realize competitive advantage and differentiate an organization from the competition. Before starting any transformational efforts, pay careful attention to collecting good and meaningful data so that suitable decisions can be made by the business and project team.

At the end of the day, it is "garbage in, garbage out"; therefore, collecting good data that is credible, meaningful, and relevant usually allows for solutions that have a higher sense of integrity. It is not only what data is gathered but also how it is gathered, how it is transformed into information, and how all of that is used to form winning decisions.

When it comes to decisions, leaders are faced with addressing them through two approaches:

- **Unstructured approach:** Apply assumptions about the situation, solutions, effectiveness, and how changes can potentially work. Basically, follow the gut feeling.

- **Structured approach:** Understand the situation, collect data, process the data to make sense of it, form an understanding, determine short- or long-term solutions, apply selection criteria, launch, and validate.

The insights gathered from customers, products, employees, competitors, the environment, and everything else can feed into a data-processing mechanism that helps the business decision makers make better solutions for their customers. After all, as W. Edwards Deming has reminded us, "without data, you're just another person with an opinion."[10]

Before the Internet boom, data was very precious. The people and businesses that had data could have significant advantage over those that did not. However, in recent years, there has been an explosion of data that is available everywhere and to everyone. With a simple Internet search, any person can have a decent amount of information about almost any topic in mind. The problem is that there are now so many resources and so much data that different data providers are creating distraction—they may not give similar outputs. It's true that "a wealth of information creates a poverty of attention," as Herbert A. Simon has said.[11]

The current mass of data available to everyone is meaningless without the ability to validate its credibility, clean it up, and make sense out of it. It is a good idea to understand the difference between data, information, knowledge, and wisdom (the DIKW pyramid). Information, for instance, consists of data, but data is not necessarily information. Also, knowledge is not necessarily wisdom, but wisdom comes from knowledge, which in turn comes from information, which is derived from data.

- **Data:** A collection of facts, numbers, characters, or figures that are usually unorganized.

- **Information:** Data that has been cleaned and processed so that it can describe something or somebody. Data processing can involve several operations, such as aggregation, which is combining different sets of data, and validation, which is ensuring that the data collected is accurate.

- **Knowledge:** When there is a good understanding of how to make sense of the information and translate it into ideas and principles, then knowledge is realized.

- **Wisdom:** Wisdom is achieved when knowledge is utilized to make decisions and judgments.

Over the years, wisdom has been uniquely connected with humans because it requires a sense of good and bad, right and wrong, and ethical and unethical. However, with advanced AI, complicated algorithms feeding computers have been able to reach a certain degree of decision making that until recently was attributed only to humans.

Artificial intelligence (AI): Computers can now be programmed to mimic human abilities and simulate human intelligence. When machines become intelligent, they can understand requests, connect data points, and draw conclusions. AI has several steps that can range from basic "what if" scenarios all the way to cognitive automation.

- **"What if" scenarios analysis (WISA):** This is a simple and powerful tool for planning and making decisions. It is used to evaluate projections or potential outcomes based on plugging in and selectively changing inputs. It enables people to understand how variables might affect the results, and potentially take action to exploit or avoid certain outcomes. In simplest forms, "what if" scenarios can be utilized using simple computer codes or even spreadsheets. "What if" scenarios don't tell the future, but they paint a picture of what the future could look like, given certain assumptions, and can help organizations plan their next steps based on key input elements.

- **Business intelligence (BI):** Traditional analysis began with basic BI, where processes, technologies, and architectures were used to transform raw historical data into information. Computer systems have evolved to offer tools and techniques to sort and filter data. Current advanced analytics tools focus on forecasting future events and behaviors to predict the effects of potential changes in business strategies. New educational degrees are now specialized in advanced data analytics to focus on projecting future trends, events, and behaviors so that organizations are given the ability and power to perform data modeling and ensure their solutions fit well with customer requirements. BI allows the access and analysis of data, then transforms it into information that analysts can use in reports, summaries, graphs, dashboards, projections, and other visual outputs.

- **Machine learning (ML):** This step specifically uses data to learn and adapt through experience in order to determine outcomes, without being explicitly programmed to do so. ML is a subset of AI but has the ability to dynamically modify itself without human intervention. ML is one of the most powerful technologies for transforming information to knowledge. There are several types of ML, including supervised, unsupervised, semi-supervised, and reinforcement.

- **Cognitive automation:** Cognitive automation is the highest level of AI, and takes automation to the next level. It brings intelligence to information-intensive processes, imitating the way humans think by using technology as lateral language, processing images, recognizing patterns, and making intuitive judgments. Cognitive automation leverages different algorithms and technologies, including ML, natural language processing (NLP), data mining, and robotic process automation (RPA). RPAs, for example, are being used to try to ease the connection and interface between different technologies, or between legacy and newer systems. They can save significant cost and time when designed correctly to replace processes that are highly manual, rule-based, and repetitive. While those tools have many times proved successful, they often come with a high cost and much monitoring and support. Therefore, proper feasibility analysis should be in place to ensure the planned AI projects offer efficient solutions worth the money invested in them.

It is important to note here that while many argue that machines are gaining ground in performing tasks and activities with much greater efficiency than humans, when it comes to strategic decisions that could make or break organizations, machines are probably no match yet to the wisdom of savvy business leaders. Human intellectual knowledge and wisdom are usually able to apply not only data to come up with decisions, but also the business sense or acumen that comes with experience and vision.

Cloud computing: Many activities related to processing data and information while applying complex processes and calculation have been commonly done by on-premise software installed in on-premise computers. Many of these "local" software programs and machines are reliable and secure, and allow organizations to maintain control. However, they can be expensive, require backups, provide limited accessibility, are at risk of breaking, and are susceptible to hacking.

Cloud computing offers the solution of using software in the cloud, which is a powerful computer in a secured location hosted by a third party. This allows companies to have only simple on-premise computers while allowing the cloud to run sophisticated software.

There are advantages and disadvantages of moving to the cloud, and that really depends on each organization's structure, size, regulatory mandates, outreach, number of users, infrastructure, and technical debt, among other factors.

In general, cloud computing can offer the following advantages:

- Efficiency: There is no need for 24/7 power surge protection, cooling expenses, or IT experts to maintain the infrastructure.

- Free capital: Instead of burdening the balance sheet by purchasing expensive software and racks of servers, cloud computing allows companies to operationally pay and expense for the service as needed in their P&L statement.

- Flexibility and scalability: Cloud-based solutions can support growing or shrinking of businesses.

- Disaster recovery: There is no need for a large investment in systems and contractors to ensure proper backups, redundancy, and recovery.

- Automatic software update: Usually the third party hosting the software handles all the regular upgrades and updates.

- Increased collaboration: Documents in the cloud can be accessed and edited in real time by many team members, avoiding back-and-forth file transfers and allowing version control.

- Access anywhere: Software and documents in the cloud can be accessed from anywhere in the world with Internet access.

- Access control: Controlling access in the cloud is usually simple and instantaneous.

- Speed and performance: Most cloud computing offers superior processing capabilities. Many 3D renderings and complicated calculation processes that used to take weeks and months via on-premise machines can take minutes or even just seconds in the cloud.

- Security: Data security is usually much stronger in the cloud, if access is properly maintained. The third-party hosting in the cloud has strong set of policies, technologies, and control to ensure hardware and software are very protected.

The main disadvantages of cloud computing fall under:

- Security and confidentiality: A cloud is just a computer always connected to the Internet. There is always the residual risk of someone gaining access to it, no matter how many controls are put in place by the host. Also, organizations should maintain solid user access management because in the cloud, improper access can spread quickly.

- Internet: The cloud is worthless without access to the Internet. When access is unavailable, not fast enough, or inconsistent, there can be major issues and hiccups while utilizing the cloud.

- Support: Not all vendors provide easy, 24/7 support within seconds, and if that is available, it can come with a high price tag.

- Downtime: Things can happen at the cloud hosting company. No company is immune from unforeseen issues. Even Amazon had a service outage in 2017.

- Cost: While the cloud offers pay-per-use service, for big organizations of tens or hundreds of thousands of employees, this may put a huge price tag on using the cloud.

Data security: Technology and networks continue to evolve every day, and data will continue to be one of the most important factors in decision making, enhancing customer experience, and gaining competitive advantage. With the amount of data that is available now or will grow in the ecosystems over the next many years, the threat of a data breach is much larger than people realize. People and businesses often underestimate the risk of a data breach, as they think that all of their sensitive data is contained and secure.

A few years ago, companies used to secure their data by keeping their devices unplugged from networks and disabling external ports. Today, almost every computer is connected, and the cloud is an essential part of any infrastructure.

IOT is also growing in popularity. IOT refers to all devices, sensors, smartphones, wearables, speakers, TVs, and hardware connected to the Internet and exchanging data with each other. Those IOTs are also vulnerable and susceptible to hacking.

In reality, probably no connected device is 100 percent secure, no matter how many firewalls and security measures are in place. Every day, there are stories about data security breaches or hacked accounts. In fact, there is a long and growing list of organizations that have learned painful firsthand lessons from data security issues. Cyber criminals nowadays have many tools that allow them to find loopholes and back doors into systems and networks. Criminals are now able to quickly monetize stolen information and intellectual property. Also, some foreign governments and organized crime rings have sophisticated tools and smart hackers who may be able to get them sensitive information to be used for their advantage.

Many people do not always use best practices to protect data. Simple things such as not opening a suspicious email or link and improperly setting up and changing passwords can expose people and their companies to vicious cyberattacks. A negligent or dissatisfied employee can expose confidential information if there are not enough safeguards to protect organizations and secure accidental or intentional access to sensitive data. Unprotected data leaves enterprises vulnerable to attack, but there are effective security measures that offer robust data protection plans across different networks and platforms. The following highlight the different states in which data should be secured:

• **Data at rest:** When data is stored in or off the network on a hard drive, flash drive, computer, or any form of storage device, it is called "data at rest." Information can be protected in several conventional ways, such as storing it on DVDs that are locked away, setting up firewalls, and maintaining the latest, updated antivirus programs.

However, those conventional practices may be penetrated by intruders if the storage spaces are accessed by unauthorized personnel or if networks are compromised. Different data security techniques can be used for "data at rest." Multilayer protection policies, location separation, and multilevel authentication can increase security. Data encryption is probably one of the best ways to ensure the security of data at rest.

• **Data in use:** "Data in use" is the active data that is accessed, viewed, processed, updated, or erased. It is more vulnerable than "data at rest" because it is accessible to those who need it. It is susceptible to many types of cyber threats depending on where it is in the system and who is using it. The more people and devices that have access to the data, the greater the risk that it can end up in the wrong hands.

Protecting "data in use" starts with controlling access and incorporating proper authentication steps to allow access to the desired users. Continuous diagnoses, monitoring, and tracking allow organizations to proactively detect suspicious activity and prevent potential threats.

- **Data in motion:** Also, referred to as "data in transit," this is data that moves from one location to another across physical locations or networks (local and cloud) via email, courier, fax, wireless networks, or any other channel. Data is most vulnerable to cyberattack while in motion. Data protection measures for in-transit data are critical, as hackers with the right tools can intercept your data while it is moving. The best way to protect "data in motion" is to transmit it through an encryption platform.

12

Who Should Be Doing This Work?

Successful business transformation, or any project at hand, relies on the collaboration and alignment of all parties involved in those projects. There are many stakeholders that can be key to the success of any initiative, but the two key groups that can make or break any project are the project sponsors and the project managers.

GOOD PROJECT SPONSORS

Transforming and optimizing an organization cannot be successful without true leaders who sponsor those programs. Typically, the primary sponsors are the senior executives who initiate projects. Employees look to senior leaders for spoken and unspoken messages about the direction the company is taking and their commitment to transforming and improving the business.

Not every senior leader is an ideal program sponsor. The following are ideal sponsor characteristics as highlighted by Prosci Change Management (prosci.com) practice:

- Is a recognized leader with applicable experience
- Has strong communication skills
- Creates engagement through passion and enthusiasm
- Is engaged and involved
- Is visible and supportive
- Is approachable and available

Many sponsors fail to position their programs for success because they simply do not correctly understand their role in that journey. They think that they can tell people to change, and they start living in a future state, while most people are still tied to and living in a current state built over months and years of practices and habits. The following are the five most common mistakes leaders or executive sponsors make:

1   They fail to remain active and visible throughout the life of the project

2   They underestimate or misunderstand the people side of change

3   They fail to communicate messages about the need for change

4   They delegate the sponsorship role and responsibilities

5   They fail to demonstrate support for the project in words and actions

The sponsor has the following primary roles in any project:

- Clarify and communicate scope: The scope of initiatives should be clear in the minds of sponsors before they kick off activities with managers and employees. Once that scope is defined and outlined, then communicating and reinforcing can take place.

- Provide resources (budget and people): The sponsors need to provide the necessary funds to kick off, plan, deliver, and finish a program. Lack of funds will put a halt to any initiative. One option is to put out an estimate with enough contingency to cover the unknown, specifically for those projects with an unknown end date or end state. Another option is to provide tiered and incremental budget approvals after each iteration. Providing the right human resources for the project is equally important, and it is a very important role sponsors must assume. Sometimes it takes tremendous effort to find those vital resources internally and externally, so a strong and inspiring sponsor is critical to getting that job done.

- Ensure schedule mandate is reasonable: Many projects fail because of unrealistic expectations related to the time of completion. But relaxing the schedule too much can mean missed opportunities for an organization. A wise sponsor ensures proper timing that is not unachievable but also not too lenient.

- Participate actively and visibly throughout the project: One common mistake sponsors make is disappearing once they've ignited the spark for change, kicked off the project, and signed the checks.

- Build a coalition of sponsorship with peers and managers: This includes not just the project organizational chart but also identifying and working with those who are being impacted by the project efforts, while maintaining not only a top-down communication approach but also a bottom-up one.

- Interact directly with employees: The interaction should focus on not only what is changing but also why it is changing now, and what is not changing.

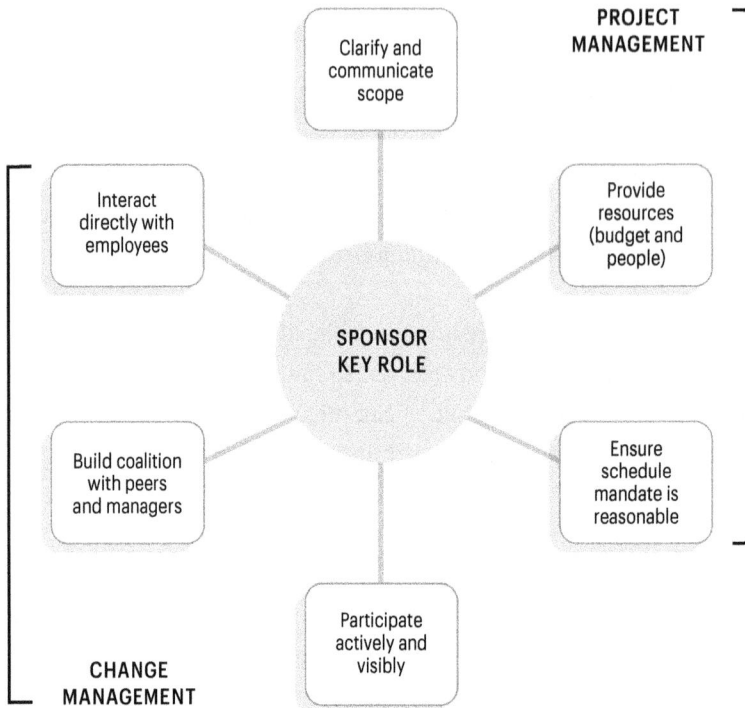

GOOD PROJECT MANAGERS

To be successful at managing a project, a manager should plan and execute that project according to the defined scope, on time and on budget. A great project manager possesses the technical capabilities and knowledge to get the job done, but also the people skills to ensure they can manage and partner with the project stakeholders.

Project management is a science and an art. Part Three of this book will dive into the communication and people skills of great leaders. The following points highlight the essential hard and soft skills that successful project managers should have.

The Science

- **Knowledgeable and experienced:** Some projects require a deep understanding of the subject matter, so the project manager needs to understand terminologies, codes, best industry practice, laws, and so on. However, great project managers can probably manage any type of project and may not need to be subject matter experts (SMEs) in certain areas. The job of project managers is simply to organize, support, facilitate, lead, coordinate, remove barriers, escalate concerns, deliver scope, and keep an eye on the budget. Usually, project managers rely on SMEs to do the technical work. By way of analogy, the master conductors may not be the best pianists or violists, but they can lead orchestras like no one else!

- **Competent:** A good project manager knows what they are doing. They are skilled in project management methodologies, tools, and best practices. They also know how to face challenges and remove impediments so the team can complete their tasks. Project managers should also have a decent amount of technical knowledge to be able to handle project planning, reporting, and action tracking.

- **Organized and focused:** Projects may be simple or complicated, small or big, but no matter what the project is about, it should be planned and executed in a well-organized fashion. Project managers should be able to demonstrate agility, discipline, organization, resilience, and common sense. Helping the team stay focused while prioritizing work and clarifying roles and responsibilities is key to the success of any project.

- **Ethical and of integrity:** When faced with tough decisions, the right decision may not be easy, but it is usually clear. Project managers should have a high degree of integrity and ethics. Being honest, taking responsibility, and protecting the company and team should always be their top priority.

The Art

- **Communicator:** Good project managers are good facilitators. They have clear communication plans and tools, and effective communication skills. Connecting with people at all levels and managing stakeholders from different backgrounds is definitely the number one objective of a project manager in order to ensure the project is delivered according to scope, on budget, and on time.

- **Leader:** Project management is pretty much a people practice. Motivating project team members and driving the planning and execution require someone of good character, who inspires people, energizes them, builds trust, cares about stakeholders, leads by example, applies empathy, and is able to do all of that while being laser-focused on the targets of the project so that it meets the objectives it was created for.

- **Calm:** Almost every project faces unforeseen events that can derail or hinder its progress. Good project managers are patient and can hold their ground without creating anxiety and causing unnecessary panic. However, if there are safety concerns, then those project managers should be acting quickly without losing themselves.

- **Courageous:** Project managers need to be fearless and task-oriented. They should be focused on actions and not be afraid to challenge the team or even executives if they feel there is something not right happening in the project.

- **Problem solver:** A seasoned project manager knows how to solve problems and make decisions. Project managers work with the team to collectively gather data, draw possibilities, find solutions, narrow down selections, and outline suggested responses. The team members should have a wealth of knowledge and experience that the project manager can utilize. Then, depending on the authority given to the project manager, they can either make a fact-based decision or recommend one to the project sponsor.

• **Negotiator:** This is particularly important from both external and internal standpoints. Externally, project managers assume or help with sourcing activities such as finding materials, resources, and contractors while negotiating best prices and scopes of work (SOW). From an internal perspective, the project team may come across many conflicts of opinions or approaches; therefore, the project manager should be skilled in settling issues and resolving conflict in order to ensure the project continues to progress as planned and meets objectives.

THE SCIENCE (HARD SKILLS)	THE ART (SOFT SKILLS)
Knowledgeable	Communicator
Experienced	Leader
Competent	Calm
Organized	Courageous
Focused	Problem solver
Ethical and of integrity	Negotiator

13

When Should We
Work on Blueprints?

I t is probably never too late for an organization to change, improve, explore new opportunities, realize new potential, or reach new dimensions.

Without risk, there will be no rewards. Organizations should sometimes get out of their comfort zone and adopt a fresh, evolving mindset that always focuses on transformation, optimization, innovation, and excellence. This includes the will and energy to "sunset" business processes and technologies that may have worked in the past but may not be suitable to address new challenges or opportunities. Postponing transformation projects can sometimes be a good strategy because technology may not be mature enough or is too expensive, or because timing is just not right. However, procrastination may haunt those organizations and could put their own future in jeopardy, because the competition is not waiting for an invitation. NHL great Wayne Gretzky has cautioned, "You miss 100 percent of the shots you don't take."[12]

There are times when companies feel a false sense of security and comfort because the economy is good and money is up for grabs. However, an inevitable economic downturn or changes in the competition dynamics can pressure-test organizations and filter out those that are not efficient and innovative. Companies should always be ahead and proactive in having their transformation road map ready. Transformation or optimization are journeys, not events. They will take much time and many resources. So, blueprints should already be figured out and efforts should already have begun.

The diagram on the next page illustrates how human beings feel when they stay in their comfort zone, when they start getting out of that comfort zone into unfamiliar territory (called the danger zone), when they push their limit far beyond those unfamiliar territories, beyond the danger zone and into a learning zone, and when they enter into a whole new growth zone. Of course, the further human beings go from their comfort zone, the more risk they take, and that can be either rewarding or harmful.

The key here is to fight fear, calculate risk, take a step forward, avoid fatal mistakes, and maneuver carefully through those danger and terror zones while trying to find new worlds of opportunity to explore and growth potential to grab. When getting out of a comfort zone, it is normal to face uncertainty and be afraid to fall. Thomas Carlyle once said: "The block of granite which was an obstacle in the pathway of the weak, became a stepping-stone in the pathway of the strong."[13]

In the comfort zone, there is a great deal of control, safety, and familiarity, but also, with low risk comes low reward. This zone feels safe, calm, peaceful, and happy.

As soon as people get out of the comfort zone, they enter a danger zone, where they start to feel fearful, unsure, stressed, hesitant, exposed, less confident, and impacted by criticism. In this stage, there is tendency to retreat to the comfort zone.

The tipping point happens when people face their fear, find solutions to their problems, acquire new skills, and build confidence as they see new opportunities; this happens in the learning zone. Usually, people start establishing new comfort zone boundaries and rebuild confidence and control. The learning zone is a place of adventure, where new benchmarks are set.

The next stage is the growth zone, where fruition happens, rewards are captured, new purpose is found, and new limits are established; this can also potentially bring new types of challenges, but people usually don't look back, and see that the path is only forward-looking.

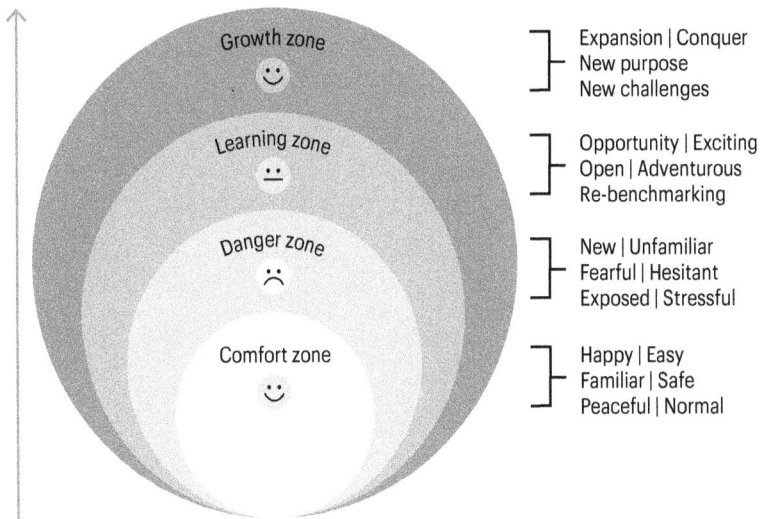

14

How Can We Position Ourselves for Success?

MANAGING EXPECTATIONS

Business transformation and optimization take time and dedication. This process is a journey, not a panacea. Patience is key when going through an optimization or a transformation journey, and resilience is a virtue. Most leaders looking to make big changes in their organizations quit too early because they think that the return is linear when it is actually exponential.

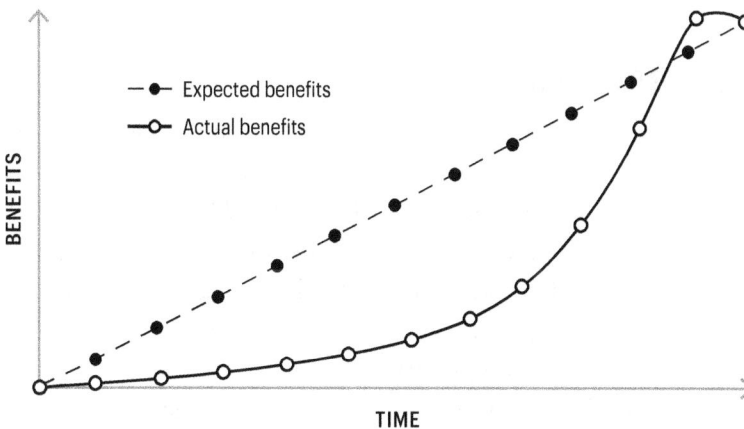

Business leaders should set expectations around priorities, benefits, efforts, and timing. Overselling or overpromising often results in failing expectations and can lead to a loss of confidence and abandonment. Priorities cannot be set in a vacuum. Transparency across functions and from different levels in the organization is key.

Also, honest feedback should be encouraged, not punished. Leaders should be receptive to feedback. Sometimes, it is necessary to give a little push and cascade down the goals and mandates, but employees should not be afraid to voice concerns and recommendations. Without that input, senior leaders may get a false sense that the way ahead is clear when, in reality, the road may be full of obstacles that will make the transformation journey unpleasant, bumpy, or even unreasonable.

Transformational efforts should lead to agreed-upon goals that are achievable but aggressive enough to gain traction. The important factor is to make sure the goals are SMART:

- **S:** Specific with exact scope and needs
- **M:** Measurable to understand effectiveness and applicability
- **A:** Achievable through actions by resources utilized
- **R:** Realistic and not out of reach while relevant to the vision
- **T:** Timed to ensure mandates do not linger and lose steam

GENERATING IDEAS

Senior leaders may want to get ideas from different levels in the organization. Especially in big organizations, employees are the ones who best know customers and suppliers. Idea generation may be limited to a sample of the crowd, the whole organization, or certain target areas. To make it fun, the employee or group with the best idea can get a prize, award, and/or recognition. If leaders are faced with resistance to come up with ideas to do things safer, better, faster, and cheaper, they can encourage the team to think about the consequences of not generating solutions, and how these consequences can impact the organization, including them, over the short or long term.

To make the idea-generating exercise useful and meaningful, the team needs to understand the focus or objective and keep focused on the scope. The facilitator should record all ideas and try not to be biased. Some of those ideas may eventually be filtered out at a later stage by the team. It is a best practice to allow individuals to complete their thoughts without interruption from other team members, and encourage everyone to build on existing ideas.

During the exercise, the team should avoid making immediate judgment on people's suggestions, whether verbal or visual, so as not to make the idea generator uncomfortable. Immediate judgment can also prevent others from coming up with bright out-of-the-box solutions. Also, the facilitator must try to discourage attendees from becoming "idea assassins" who usually find a problem for every solution and challenge every assumption—the objective is to find a solution for every problem. Finally, the moderator should try to give everyone in the group a chance to make suggestions, and try to discourage any one person or group from dominating the session.

When it comes to generating ideas, business leaders may utilize different techniques to collect and validate suggestions that could turn into initiatives to potentially help optimize or transform organizations. The following are some idea-generating tools:

- **Brainstorming:** The main objective of brainstorming meetings is to generate as many ideas as possible. Brainstorming can take different forms:

  - Round robin: This technique involves moving around the group to allow every team member to present an idea.

  - Shout out: Any team member can shout out an idea as it comes to their mind; then anyone can build on that idea.

  - Silent: To try reducing the impact of dominant personalities in the room, a silent technique can be used: members write ideas on slips of paper and give them to the moderator, who then reveals them and allows for discussion and evaluation.

- **Survey:** If there is a large number of participants in the idea-generating activity, surveys can be created and sent to participants by email, via online avenues, or on paper. Survey output can be analyzed to find the best ideas with the most potential benefits.

- **Interviewing:** Interviews can be conducted with individuals or certain groups so they have the freedom and privacy to say what they want without the fear of being judged or challenged by other team members or supervisors.

- **Historical data/events:** Business leaders can research past success stories, turning points, or events that happened or are happening in the organization, other entities, sister companies, or even competitor companies. Learning from mistakes and building on success stories can be a very effective tool in coming up with bright ideas.

- **Benchmarking:** Organizations may look for opportunities by benchmarking and comparing themselves against other leaders in the industry, successful competitors, or even nichers that are specialized in certain markets.

- **Industry experts or SMEs:** Consulting agencies, industry professionals, or SMEs can provide a wealth of knowledge and ideas because they know the market, product, or area very well. They may have access to information that is hard to obtain. Of course, this can come with a high price tag, but it may be able to save the company weeks or months of efforts.

- **Research:** Magazines, videos, keynotes, summits, articles, lessons learned from other industries or experts, online posting, and blogs are just some samples of tools available for research and coming up with ideas.

- **Reverse thinking:** Instead of thinking about how to reach the company's goals, the team can think about how not to achieve them and what could cause the company to fail. Sometimes, this technique enables the team to come up with many unconventional solutions.

- **Blue-sky dreaming:** Ask team members: "If you had a magic wand, what would you wish the company would do?" or, "If money were not a problem, what would you wish the company could get?"

- **Other:** There are many other tools and methods to generate ideas, such as SCAMPER, role playing, storyboarding, and so on.

PRIORITIZATION AND SELECTION

Companies can be faced with many options when it comes to making decisions about business strategies, tactics, or even actions. Business leaders may be able to use one or more of several techniques to aid decision making, such as:

- **Nominal group technique (NGT):** During a brainstorming session, each member of the group presents an opinion on what the best ideas are and why. The ideas that are redundant are eliminated, and then the team ranks the remaining ones.

- **Delphi technique:** The team aims to find fewer options by asking a facilitator to compile the ideas at hand. Then they take the remaining options and try to find the best one. If the team cannot agree on a decision, the facilitator tries to repeat the process by further condensing the list of choices and presenting again to the team for further consideration.

- **Voting:** If a decision about the best ideas can be achieved by a simple yes or no answer, then the team can do a vote. This option is popular when the ideas are easy to understand.

- **Ranking:** This is similar to voting but instead of a yes or no answer, the team members assign a number based on one or more criteria to each idea and then rank them to determine the best options.

- **Pros and cons list:** The team can list the pros and cons of each option and put them side by side. Then, by evaluating the quantity and impact of those advantages and disadvantages, the team can reach a decision about the best options to pick.

- **PICK chart:** PICK is an abbreviation for Possible, Implement, Challenge, and Kill. The team can give each idea a score based on how much effort it needs and the benefits it produces. The idea is then placed in a quadrant based on the Benefits/Effort score. If the idea takes too much effort and produces few benefits, then it should be killed. If it generates many benefits and does not need too much effort, then it is low-hanging fruit and should be implemented. If it requires little effort but produces little benefit, then the team can discuss if it is possible and worth doing. If the idea requires much effort but would potentially generate many benefits, then the team can evaluate if it is feasible to do.

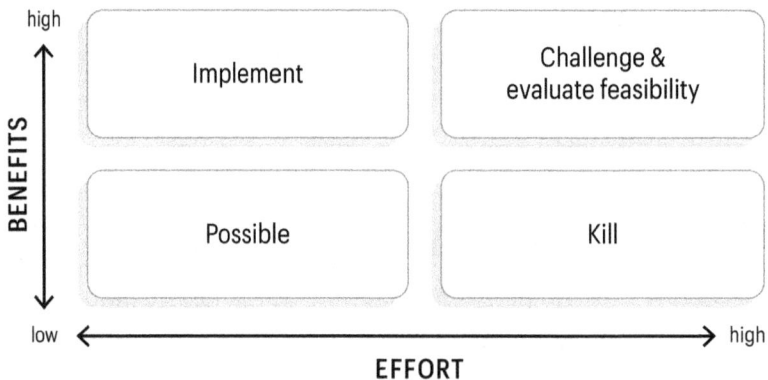

KEEP IT SIMPLE

Confucius said, "Do not use a cannon to kill a mosquito!" and that's often a challenge when deciding on a problem-solving approach.

Business leaders are usually overachievers and type A people. They pride themselves on their problem-solving skills, so they sometimes fall into the trap of ignoring the right option when it is too obvious. To prove their worth, solidify status, or hit on their superior intelligence, they tend at times to make things look complicated and difficult so they can build smart solutions to resolve issues. However, most of the time, the simplest solution or approach is usually the most effective and correct answer to any issue. Organizations should beware of overcomplicating the work or processes, as sometimes "less is more"—the focus should be on what truly matters. Simple, straight-forward solutions are much easier to explain, understand, scale, measure, and adopt. After all, as Albert Einstein said, "if you can't explain it simply, you don't understand it well enough."[14]

The following are some of the best practices to think about when planning and enabling business transformation, or any work for that matter:

- Resources and time are very precious; do not waste them.

- Avoid overloading an organization with too many initiatives. This causes budget overburden, a loss of focus, and a high level of anxiety and frustration among employees.

- Do not overcomplicate or overanalyze. Instead, plan in the right amount, take action, create a tracker, and inspire people while holding them accountable for delivering the actions to which they're assigned.

- Do not wait for perfection! Try to deliver incremental value, and quickly, before opportunities are lost. Be nimble; learn how to think and move fast.

- Do not pass the hot potato. If a tough mission appears ahead, create an action plan and get the right people to help address it immediately, before it creates more problems.

- Keep a RAID log: Risks, Actions, Issues, and Decisions. The log is quite handy and ensures no gaps are left unfilled.

- Try to avoid Band-Aids when possible; do not use a short-term fix on a long-term problem.

- Do not assume you know your customers. Instead, continually listen to them and to internal and external critics.

- Do not bet on consumer loyalty; in today's environment, customers will quickly switch when they find a better alternative. Therefore, be flexible and innovative.

- Do not fool yourself, and be aware of "superficial improvement." Make sure your improvements are real by establishing KPIs, or tracking them in the financial statements.

- Aim to move from push to pull. In other words, you can push your products, services, or strategies, but ultimately, you want your customers or stakeholders to "pull" or ask for them.

- Avoid gold plating: Do not give customers way more than they asked for, or, "Do not try to paint everything with gold." The extra effort and the money spent may not be worth it or appreciated.

- Be aware of any scope creep and avoid shiny objects that distract you from reaching your true goal.

- Do not be afraid to stop initiatives if they no longer fit the overall objectives of the organization.

- Put in place sunset criteria for each initiative so that a definitive closure happens when the deliverables are met.

- Do not give up! Small steps lead to giant leaps.

15

How Much Did We Spend?

Tracking spending during any project or business journey is very important. The worst thing a team can face is running out of money midcourse, just like running out of fuel in the desert while driving from one city to another. Cost tracking and staying on top of the project budget is one of the most difficult tasks a project manager has to do. Whether it is a small project or a big transformation program, the project leader should help in estimating cost, tracking spending, and reporting budget status to the business leaders.

The following are key activities and tactics that are helpful in establishing and tracking budgets:

1. Cost estimation: The first step is to complete an estimation of how much the project will cost. This estimation should not be overly optimistic or pessimistic, and needs to be realistic enough to allow the project to be delivered on scope and on schedule. Different projects require different types of cost, but the following are examples of items that can be considered during cost estimation: hardware, software, materials, equipment, supplies, contractors, licensing, subscriptions, fuel, travel, food and beverages, entertainment, and human resources (internal and external). It is advisable to add a buffer or contingency amount to account for any unexpected events. Usually the buffer is between 10 and 20 percent of the total project budget. The estimation process can take days, weeks, or months depending on the availability of information and sources of goods or materials. The project team often goes through a bidding process, sending RFPs or RFQs in order to get the best proposals or prices for their companies.

2. Funding: After the estimation is done by the project team, they need to take it to the business sponsor to get it approved and funded. The request for funds should include a disbursement plan on when they need the money, because it is highly unlikely that the funds will be given to the team all at once at the beginning of the project. Thus, the business leaders should be aware of approximately how much is needed and when so that they can have the right amount in cash in the bank or ready to be transferred to the right vendors.

3. Controls: Establishing controls on who is authorized to spend the money and how many different levels of employees are allowed to spend is important. Protecting the company's money is a priority. The project leader should help the business leaders establish and approve cost controls regarding who has what permission to spend the money. Different types of spending may need different levels of signatures and permissions. For example, the authority to sign off on and pay a multimillion-dollar or multiyear contract should be given to senior executives, while the approval of time sheets and office supplies can be handled by the project managers. Also, as part of the budget control, the project leaders should identify and communicate to the team the mechanism to submit their expenses, the codes they need to use, and the supporting documents they must provide. All of this should be audited on a regular basis to ensure compliance with the mandates outlined by the company's policy.

4. Monitoring spending: The team should have a system to extract reports on how much money has been spent during the project's life cycle. Usually, a monthly report is generated to show all the expenses by category (supplies, equipment, resources, travel, etc.). The project manager must always compare what has been spent versus what is in the budget, and also establish an updated forecast to ensure that the project has enough funds to last till all the scope is delivered. Generally, the Project Management Institute's Project Management Body of Knowledge (PMI PMBOK) suggests that the following elements be frequently reported to track project budget:

- Budget at completion (BAC): The total budget for the whole project or program.

- Present value (PV = BAC × planned percentage completed) also sometimes called budgeted cost to date (BC): The budgeted cost of work scheduled to date. In theory, PV would equal BAC at the end of a project, or, it is BAC × 100 percent.

- Earned value (EV = BAC × actual percentage completed): The budgeted cost of work performed to date. That work performed may be less or more than the work scheduled.

- Schedule variance (SV = EV - PV): The amount of money representing work performed versus work planned. If SV equals zero, then the work is going according to schedule. If it is positive, then the project is progressing ahead of schedule. If SV is negative, then the project is running behind schedule.

- Schedule performance index (SPI = EV / PV): If this index equals 1, then the work is going according to schedule. If it is higher than 1, then the project is progressing ahead of schedule. If SPI is less than 1, then the project is running behind schedule.

- Actual cost to date (AC): The money that has been spent to date on the project.

- Cost variance ($CV = EV - AC$): If CV equals zero, then the project is currently on budget. If it is positive, then the project is currently within budget. If CV is negative, then the project is currently over budget and leaders need to be prepared to authorize additional funds if they want to complete the project per scope, or they can cut some of the scope mandates to bring CV to zero.

- Cost performance index ($CPI = EV / AC$): If this index equals 1, then the project is currently on budget. If it is more than 1, then the project is currently under budget. If the CPI is less than 1, then the project is currently over budget and leaders need to be prepared to authorize additional funds if they want to complete the project per scope, or they can cut some of the scope mandates to bring CPI to 1.

- Estimate to complete ($ETC = [BAC - EV] / [CPI \times SPI]$): How much money the team thinks they need to finish the job.

- Estimate at completion ($EAC = AC + ETC$): Actual cost plus estimate to complete.

- Variance at completion ($VAR = BAC - EAC$): Total project budget minus EAC. If this amount is zero, then the project is estimated to finish according to budget. If VAR is positive, then the project is estimated to finish below budget. If VAR is negative, then the project is likely to be over budget and leaders need to be prepared to authorize additional funds if they want to complete the project per scope, or they can cut some of the scope mandates to bring VAR to zero.

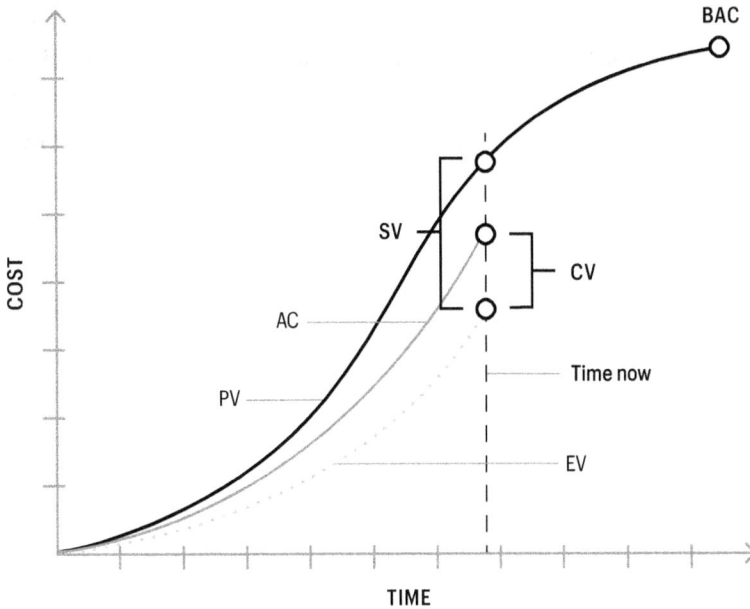

5. Report out: It is the duty of the project manager to generate and share budget tracking reports with the sponsors and other business leaders to provide visibility on budget status and ensure transparency on how much money has been spent, what is left, and how much more is needed. Project cost can be treated differently based on project types and accounting treatments. For example, some costs may be treated as capital expense (CAPEX) (they go on the balance sheet and are depreciated over a number of years) or operational expense (OPEX) (they go in the P&L as cost to be realized in a specific month). Reporting can take many forms, such as in a burnup (or burndown) format showing a cumulative budget baseline and a cumulative actual and forecasted trend line. Once the actual spend line touches the budget line, then alerts should be given that there is a potential budget overrun. However, there are times when a project can spend a lot of money in a single period and have lighter spending in another period. The project manager should always have a close eye on the budget and document spending, and accurately report the budget status on a regular basis to the project sponsors and business leaders. The following is a sample of a burnup chart that is helpful in tracking progressive actual spending, how it compares to the budget, and if the projected forecast is going to meet or be over or under budget.

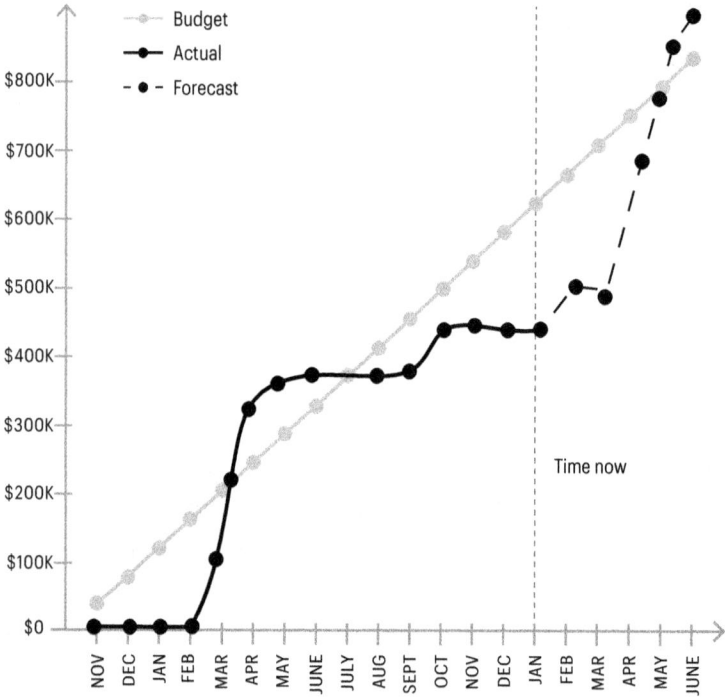

In Part Two, I covered the importance of an action-oriented mindset, the delivery mechanism, project management, data, and tracking progress. We formed a good understanding of not only coming up with plans but also taking action, being persistent, and delivering plans according to the predefined scope, budget, and timeline. In Part Three, I will shed light on the importance of culture and how organizations can change their people, develop capabilities, and embrace change through change management.

Why we are not successful even though we have an amazing strategy and business delivery mechanism?

Why is it taking so long to reach our destination?

Why are our people unable or unwilling to adapt to changes we are making?

Why is our employee turnover rate (ETR) so high?

Why are our competitors able to recruit better employees faster than us?

PART THREE

CULTURE, CAPABILITIES, AND CHANGE MANAGEMENT

16

Why Should the "People" Aspect Keep Us Up at Night?

Change is not easy, but not changing can be fatal. People resist change because it comes with uncertainty—in this case, new processes and environments that are unfamiliar. One of the most challenging aspects businesses face when trying to deliver their objectives is changing their people fast enough to adapt to changes in the business environment or changes caused by business initiatives such as transformation and optimization.

Many times, business leaders mistakenly associate project success with technical success. Soon enough, these leaders realize that if people do not support, engage, and be part of the change, then the benefits of any initiatives will be delayed and/or not fully realized. A study by Prosci shows that with high change management effectiveness, initiatives are six times more likely to meet and exceed objectives, one and a half times more likely to be delivered within budget, and five times more likely to be on schedule.[15]

The ADKAR model for change management presented by Prosci is powerful, as it outlines the five sequential phases for how to achieve change by changing people:[16]

- **A (Awareness):** In this phase, leaders should provide employees with information on the need to change, what is changing, when change is happening, and the plan to address that change. Without this awareness and communication, employees start to assume, ask questions, spread rumors, and experience increased anxiety. Typically, what leaders should aim for in this phase is to hear the following: "I understand why this is happening, why it is important, why it is necessary..."

- **D (Desire):** This is where leaders inspire desire among employees to support change by explaining what the benefits are for the organization and what's in it for them as employees. Then they can engage them while allowing them to participate in the decision making, if possible, to increase their productivity and accelerate adoption. What leaders love to hear after this phase from their employees is: "I have decided to support, to act, to engage, to help..."

- **K (Knowledge):** Here is where people start to know how to change and learn new skills, processes, tools, technologies, and behaviors. Education, training, coaching, mentoring, and job shadowing are some examples of learning techniques utilized in this phase. Knowledge increases not only the likelihood of adopting to change, but also productivity. Leaders after this phase want to hear things like: "I know how to do this, I understand how to use this..."

- **A (Ability):** This is the most critical phase of all. At this point, employees should be able to implement the required skills, processes, tools, technologies, and behaviors. At this specific phase, organizations are able to reach their desired change management objectives. This is when change really starts to happen, objectives start to be met, and values start to be realized. Ability is different from knowledge.

To illustrate, a person can read twenty-five books on how to perform the perfect open-heart surgery and can acquire the knowledge that is needed to operate on a real person. However, probably nobody would want to be under that person's knife to have such surgery! The ability to actually perform the surgery requires years of training, experience, practice, and coaching. After this phase, leaders should expect to hear something like: "I am able to do this, I am confident in my ability to perform this…"

- **R (Reinforcement):** This is where people should be reminded of the change priorities and consequences of not changing. Sustaining the change and ensuring that employees do not revert to their old ways of working is critical because new habits take time and patience. In this phase, leaders want to hear something like: "I will continue to do this, I will make sure to keep doing this…"

A common mistake project and business leaders make is not paying close attention to change management early in their project or transformation journey. They usually become too technical in the scope, road map, and results without considering the people aspect. Typically, they realize the need to start engaging people only at advanced stages in the journey, and then try to catch up by rushing to do change management at the eleventh hour. However, the right approach is to align the project management and change management phases from the beginning to ensure smoother sailing to the finish line and realize the desired outcomes.

Effective project management helps set processes, utilize best practices, and put tools in place to develop and implement change in a structured way, to achieve a defined scope that adds value to the organization. Effective change management maximizes the speed of change adoption while avoiding productivity loss and employee turnover as projects are initiated, planned, and executed.

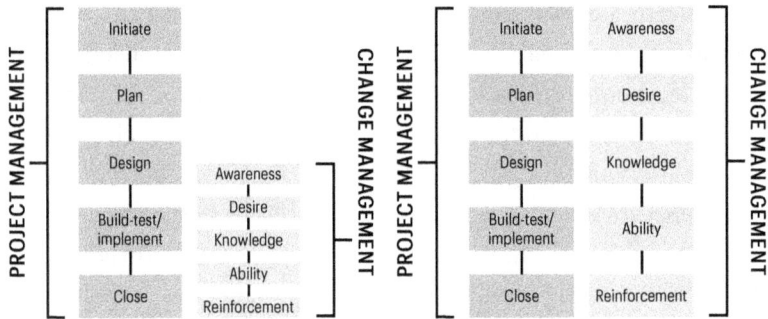

The alignment between project and change management results in a reduction of rework, less confusion for customers and employees, and ultimately realizing benefits faster.

Habits in organizations are notoriously sticky, so in order for leaders to enable change and allow people to embrace it, they need to start by preparing for change, then managing change, and, finally, reinforcing change. Here is a quick overview of some activities that are done during each of these phases:

• **Preparing for change:** Preparing for transformation within an organization includes conducting readiness assessments, performing risk analysis, completing group impact analysis, anticipating areas of resistance, designing special tactics, developing overall strategy, architecting team structure, preparing the change management team, and assessing sponsorship for competency.

• **Managing change:** This is when the change management planning and activities happen. The main activities include creating several plans—one each for communication, sponsorship, coaching, resistance management, and training. Once those plans are in place, they need to be integrated with the project plan in alignment with the project management team. After that, executing the plans can begin.

- **Reinforcing change:** Ensuring the change is adopted and sustained is ultimately the main goal of the change management work. For that to happen, the following activities can be performed: Proactively collecting feedback and listening to the people, auditing compliance to ensure the new ways are in place, identifying gaps, implementing any corrective actions needed, and finally, celebrating success!

Change management focuses on the "people side" (the "who") of organizational change. Often, this important element is easily missed by business leaders, as they tend to focus on the technical aspects, assuming that people will automatically adopt the changes and follow. Change management requires involvement and actions by business leaders in any organization (the "how").

Too often, companies do not communicate properly. Or, worse, they just assume everyone already knows what they are supposed to do and when. Leaders and employees should always be speaking a common language that aligns with the business' vision and objectives.

Change is often seen as ambiguous and difficult to understand. Therefore, leaders should make it easy to understand. When leaders' messages about change are inconsistent, ambiguity and confusion in the organization surface. However, when themes such as clear communication and inclusivity become part of the organization's change management practice, change can solidify.

Numerous negative consequences can arise when change management is not correctly put in place to get people on board. The following are some examples of those potential problems:

- Lower productivity
- Passive and active resistance
- Turnover of good employees
- Loss of interest in the organization's vision
- Increased use of sick days, or employees not showing up for work
- Obstacles are created in the interest of reverting back to how things were
- Staff try to slow down or prevent change from occurring
- Band-Aids and workarounds are used instead of facing issues head-on
- Friction by those who are with and against change, creating a culture of two poles within the organization
- Loss of morale, support, and enthusiasm

17

What Should We Focus On?

In order for any organization to be successful in delivering its objectives, it should focus on improving its culture and investing in people's capabilities. Good business leaders always strive to find the right balance between advancing their organizations to compete in the marketplace and creating an environment in which their people feel appreciated. One of the most important elements of a business is its people. Any business strategy is only as good as the people implementing it; the people are only as good as the culture allows them to be; and the culture is only as good as the leaders who formed it.

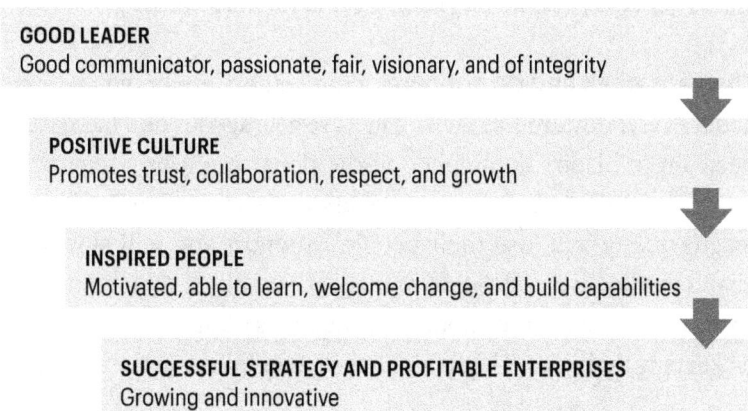

GOOD LEADER
Good communicator, passionate, fair, visionary, and of integrity

POSITIVE CULTURE
Promotes trust, collaboration, respect, and growth

INSPIRED PEOPLE
Motivated, able to learn, welcome change, and build capabilities

SUCCESSFUL STRATEGY AND PROFITABLE ENTERPRISES
Growing and innovative

GOOD LEADERS

Why is good leadership so important? Leaders are hired to position organizations for success. They form strategies, drive execution, address customers' needs, and deliver the value that is expected by the company's owners or shareholders. However, business leaders cannot do this alone. They need people to help them achieve the company's objectives. Some leaders are lucky enough to join organizations that already have a good culture and good people, but how to maintain and continuously improve is also a leader's priority. Some leaders are tasked to build a good culture to lure and recruit good people, which is not an easy task in today's competitive work environment.

Leaders must always build and sustain a healthy corporate culture that encourages good employees to join, add value, grow, and potentially become leaders themselves. The energy and character of a leader not only cascades down to every level below that leader, but also creates a halo effect among all the other leaders and stakeholders around them. Many leaders fail to achieve that rapport with and respect from their employees and other leaders in the organization. The following are some reasons managers fail at being good leaders:

- **They lack vision:** Foggy thoughts, unclear objectives, and myopic thinking cause employees and senior leaders to lose confidence in the leader. It is not enough for leaders to be good stewards and keep status quo; they should be visionary and forward-looking.

- **They are weak and do not care:** True leaders are brave and care about everybody around them. They are courageous and face issues head-on to inspire confidence in the department or company. If bosses are selfish and do not care about their employees and colleagues, they will lose their people's support and will slowly be abandoned or avoided. Some managers care about their status and spans of control but not about the company's future; they focus only on keeping their jobs. That is also a recipe for failure in the long term.

- **They are moody and inconsistent:** These behaviors quickly lead to a loss of confidence and trust among the team and others.

- **They cannot motivate their team:** Igniting motivation and keeping the team inspired to deliver ambitious results are key factors in successful leadership. Unmotivated employees drag their feet to work and do not have the energy to help the organization.

- **They are arrogant:** This is a defensive display that occurs in response to low self-confidence; the leader tries to overstate their sense of superiority and disparages others. A true leader is confident but also humble and down-to-earth.

- **They are untrustworthy or deceitful:** Lying and stabbing others in the back destroys confidence, faith, trust, and morale in organizations. Trust is usually binary: people either trust or do not trust others. Do not expect a person to trust someone 80 percent, for example. Once trust is gone, it is very hard to regain it.

- **They are worried about being popular:** A big mistake some leaders make is trying to make themselves available everywhere, part of every action, and trying to please everybody. Everyone wants to be liked; however, that should be shown via results and actions, not by being a people pleaser or showing up in every meeting even if not needed. True leaders trust their employees to act on their behalf and get work done properly. They are also not afraid to hold people accountable and exert pressure if needed while calling out risks and mistakes, even when it may not please others.

- **They do not empower people:** Trying to manage everything oneself is a big mistake. First, leaders are by no means infallible—doing it all doesn't mean all of it will be done right. Second, such a workload also causes leaders to miss or create errors. And third, leaders who do not empower their people are often viewed as selfish and untrusting.

- **They take all the credit:** When things go well, some leaders focus on demonstrating how good they are rather than praising their team members for a job well done. Moving away from the "I" to the "we" is the first defining character of a true leader.

- **They pass blame:** When things go wrong, bad bosses do not have the courage to admit mistakes. Instead, they point fingers in different directions in an effort to find someone else to blame for their failure.

- **They do not take ownership:** Many bosses try to avoid difficult tasks because they are afraid of failure. A true leader takes ownership and leads by example; they show their employees and colleagues that they can own a project, deliver it, and take responsibility for it.

- **They are demeaning:** Some leaders are unappreciative and make condescending comments directly or indirectly. They explicitly say things to employees or colleagues that cause demoralization in the department or company. Or, they use humor and passive-aggressiveness, causing discomfort, friction, and grudges in the workplace. Good employees often quickly seek a better environment elsewhere.

- **They are unfair and practice favoritism:** This act creates friction and jealousy among employees in a department and/or company. Some bosses have "pet employees," to whom they give the best assignments, more vacation days, highest bonuses, and frequent promotions. However, being fair and kind allows a leader to gain wide respect and trust in the organization.

- **They are unethical:** The worst thing to be in the workplace is unethical. Honesty, truthfulness, and good principles inspire trust, confidence, and security among the people surrounding a manager. Practicing unethical behavior may cause harm not only to an employee or the manager, but also to the whole company.

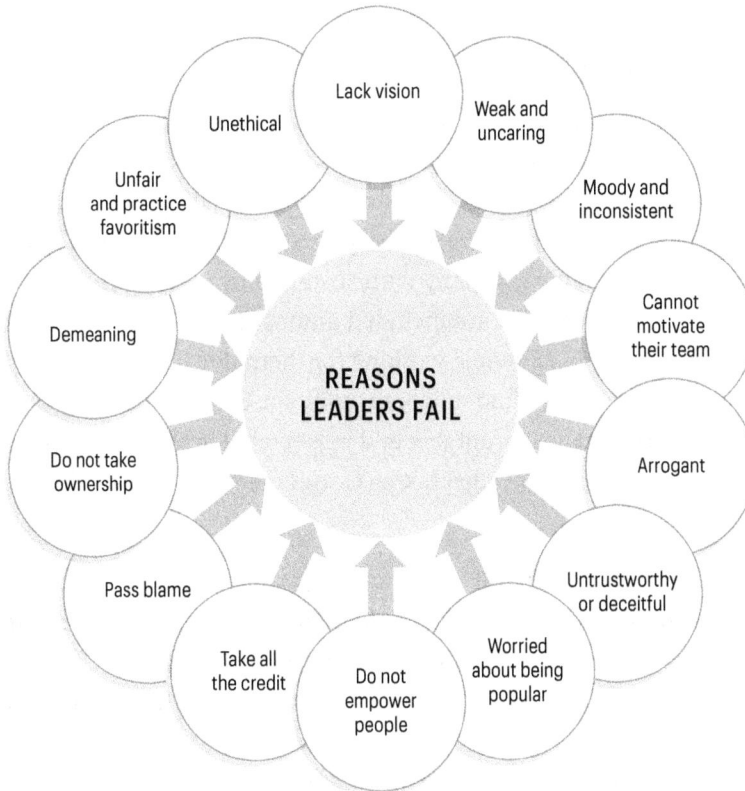

Employees look up to a good leader; peers are energized by a good colleague; and owners or shareholders seek a leader to trust with their money and organization. True leaders build good cultures that contribute to building successful organizations. One or more of the behaviors or traits outlined above can cause a leader to lose the opportunity to successfully lead an organization, department, or project.

POSITIVE CULTURE

No strategy can be executed if corporate culture does not support it. Culture is the foundation that supports the entire structure of an organization. A healthy and positive workplace starts with identifying candidates for recruiting, promoting, keeping employees satisfied, serving customers, enabling a vision, and delivering value to the company's owners or shareholders.

Companies these days race to show that they are the best place to work, sharing on media, social media, and specialty websites like Glassdoor. The reason this is so important is that there is a strong positive correlation between being "a great place to work" and being "a profitable company with sustainable competitive advantage." Companies that are included among the top places to work not only have good people working for them and competing good candidates trying to find an opportunity for employment, but also usually are the most profitable and respectable in the marketplace. Those companies know that taking care of customers starts with taking care of employees.

Competitors can virtually copy anything an organization has except for its culture. No matter what products or services are offered by the company, competitors can probably find a way to deliver a better or at least similar offering to customers. It is the culture that is the most difficult to replicate—the collective appreciation of the people within a company for their leaders, which translates to customer appreciation for whatever the company is offering and how they are treated by the company's employees during any stage in the customer journey, which in turn translates to appreciation from the market, analysts, and shareholders. It is a complete chain of appreciation.

The company's culture should ultimately inspire employees to be customer-centric and work toward the organization's goals. To create this positive culture, business leaders may want to focus on the following areas:

Create a purpose: To build a positive work culture, it is important to align the company's vision and strategy with employees' objectives and career goals. Many employees don't want to only collect a paycheck; they also need to feel a sense of purpose and meaning in their work. Their purpose could be satisfying customers, reducing pollution, or making children smile. Leaders should give employees specific examples of how their roles in the company positively impact the customers, environment, and community.

Create measurable objectives: The overall purpose of the company can be broken down into goals for each function, department, and employee. Clear goals should be in place and should be measured frequently to ensure that they still align with the company's strategy.

Create a positive culture: Positivity is contagious. It can be felt throughout a workplace in offices and at workstations and in the atmosphere in general—even over the phone. Optimism, smiles, appreciation, fair treatment, respect—these are all indicators of a positive work culture.

Communicate and be transparent: Communication is probably one of the most important factors in creating a good culture. When employees are engaged and kept in the loop, they feel appreciated and part of the company. Newsletters, town halls, regular emails from the top leaders, having an interactive intranet site, and even mobile applications are good vehicles through which a company can pass on the latest updates and exciting news, or even try to provide comfort in difficult times.

Encourage health and wellness: For organizations to have a good culture, they need to have healthy employees who feel their best physically, emotionally, and mentally in and outside of the office. Companies can subsidize sport club membership, ensure employees have regular checkups and avoid sickness, provide health and wellness consultations, and offer a clean, comfortable, and ergonomic working environment.

Provide care: When business leaders care about their employees, those employees feel appreciated and motivated. That lifts the energy in the workspace and allows for employees to give their best in return for that good faith from their leaders.

Establish a zero tolerance policy: Protecting their people and the company is one of the most important jobs of business leaders. Employees' rights must be protected. Employees should not be punished for speaking out if they see something is not right at work. Employees should know who to call and how to access resources needed to help in case they come across misconduct or unpleasant, unethical, or harassing behavior from coworkers, managers, or even customers.

Listen to feedback and take actions: Nobody is perfect, and everyone can benefit from constructive feedback. Employees love when they know their leaders listen to them and have action plans to address their candid feedback. They feel like part of an organization that values their opinion to make things better every day. Employees who feel unheard and dismissed, and who do not care about the company or customers as a result, negatively impact organization culture. Strong positive culture is built on transparent and open communication.

Clarify roles and responsibilities: A good culture starts with establishing and communicating what employees' roles and responsibilities are. Not only does this eliminate confusion and misconception among people, but it also avoids stepping on each other's toes, which can lead to conflict and bad experiences.

Celebrate successes: This opportunity is often missed: people become so wrapped up in getting jobs done that they forget to celebrate when things go right, along with the people who went above and beyond to ensure success. This can simply take the form of a small celebration in the department, a thank-you card, a lunch or dinner, a small gift, or just a genuine pat on the back. Employees love appreciation events and remember them for months and years to come. Celebrating success is a crucial part of creating a positive culture.

Encourage work–life balance: Now more than ever, employees seek balance between work and life. They understand work is necessary to pay the bills and advance their career, but they do not want that to jeopardize the rest of their life. Business leaders need to ensure that they are not putting too much of a burden on employees and expecting them to work long hours frequently. This does not mean that work should always be a walk in the park, but it also should not mean seventy-plus hours of work a week, every week. Time should be given to employees to rest, rejuvenate, take a vacation, and enjoy life with their loved ones.

Show appreciation: Good business culture always emphasizes gratitude. Business leaders should remind their employees of how appreciative they are to have them on their team and when they are doing a good job. As a result, employees become motivated to give their best at work in a friendly, healthily competitive environment. Awards may be given in monetary or nonmonetary forms, but they are a very small token of appreciation that can boost positivity in the corporate culture.

Encourage social connection: A good work culture feels like a kind of family, where people know and appreciate each other. Employees probably spend an equal amount of time with their work family as with their home family. A positive company culture depends on employees interacting with their colleagues and knowing them relatively well. Having fun at work and with coworkers makes the job environment more pleasant and engaging. Regular team dinners or lunches, picnics, fundraising activities, or even helping a local charity together are some great examples of events that can create a social bond between employees.

Promote diversity and inclusion: This is a very powerful element of success in the workplace. Promoting and implementing diversity and inclusion practices adds value to companies and boosts positivity. Welcoming people from all backgrounds and allowing them to grow and be appreciated no matter what their sex, gender, religion, sexual orientation, age, color, or ability helps create an enriching atmosphere and positive work culture. Diversity has also proved to help the bottom line. It broadens the vision and creates a business that better represents the world around us, which eventually results in more profitable and sustainable business.

GOOD CULTURE

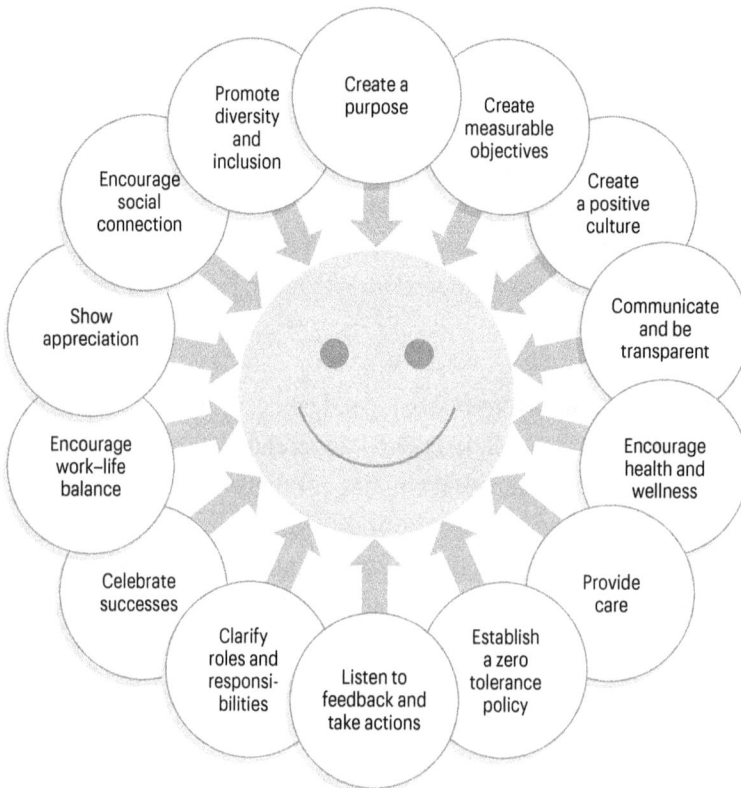

DEVELOPING EMPLOYEES' CAPABILITIES

Succeeding in operating a business, including optimization and transformation initiatives, requires more than the will and energy of employees; it also requires building and enhancing internal capabilities and harnessing talent development.

Great companies continuously upgrade the knowledge and capabilities of their employees to align with technological advancement, changes in the marketplace, and the latest best practices in the industry. The culture element, which is built and nourished by good leaders, ignites passion in employees. That passion is to come to work every day looking forward to adding value, being part of a winning organization, and finding purpose that inspires them to deliver great results. Leadership then needs to build discipline and resilience through an action-oriented mindset. This strong combination of passion, resilience, and discipline motivates people to always seek improvement and drive actions to achieve better results.

Building capabilities in this era may be different from what human beings did over the past few hundred years of accumulated learning. People should consider challenging some of the things they have learned, assess if the education is suitable for the current era, and figure out what new skills and techniques they should adapt or add in order to stay current with or even ahead of the accelerated changes in the environment. "The illiterate of the twenty-first century," Alvin Toffler has told us, "will not be those who cannot read and write, but those who cannot learn, unlearn, and relearn."[17]

Some experts claim that a decent percentage of what people are learning today in schools or at their jobs will be obsolete in a decade or two. The pace of change in this new, boundaryless world is accelerating exponentially due to changes in technology and globalization.

In the not-so-distant past, students aimed simply to get their undergraduate degree and maybe their master's, get a job or become an entrepreneur, and advance in their career or grow their own business. Somewhere along the line, many people lose interest in or their passion for learning. Soon enough, a new generation of people who are technology-savvy or more up-to-date in general start getting the new, higher-paying jobs, while the previous generation of work-age people struggle to find opportunities as their skillsets become obsolete. This happened with baby boomers and Generation X, and it continues to happen between those generations and millennials. (For reference, baby boomers are those born between 1944 and 1964; Generation X are those born between 1965 and 1979; and millennials (or Generation Y) are those born between 1980 and 1994.)

What people need to understand in today's world is that delaying the adoption of change and refusing to unlearn and relearn may cause them to lose ground quickly to the emerging workforce. Many professional accreditations nowadays mandate that their certified professionals regularly sign up for courses and even tests every year to enforce continuing education in order to keep their designation status. Businesses should not be any different in that sense. Leaders should have a mandate in their own organizations to encourage their employees to stay up-to-date with the latest innovations and updates in their industry or practices.

It is important to note that learning is not only listening to lectures and reading books. It is much more than that. Through a powerful illustration called the Cone of Experience, Edgar Dale, who was an American educator, explains how learners retain information. Illustrated on the next page, this learning pyramid is self-explanatory and shows how much information is retained and observed by people when they are exposed to different types of learning.

According to Dale's research, the least effective method of learning involves the intake of information through reading, hearing, or observing. The most effective method of learning involves active, two-directional experiences—collecting and then practicing or dispensing of the information. The Cone of Experience, also called the Cone of Learning, shows the proposed average retention rate for various methods of teaching.[18]

The conclusion is that people remember more from doing than from observing. Active learning, where people practice and do the work themselves, results in much higher information retention than inactive learning, such as being told or shown how to do the work.

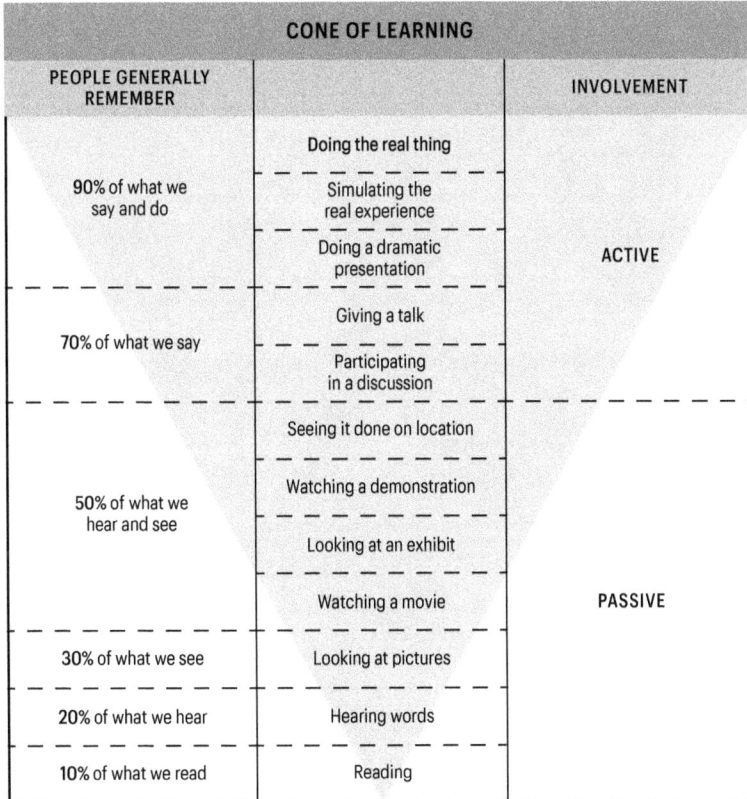

CONE OF LEARNING		
PEOPLE GENERALLY REMEMBER		INVOLVEMENT
	Doing the real thing	
90% of what we say and do	Simulating the real experience	
	Doing a dramatic presentation	ACTIVE
70% of what we say	Giving a talk	
	Participating in a discussion	
	Seeing it done on location	
50% of what we hear and see	Watching a demonstration	
	Looking at an exhibit	
	Watching a movie	PASSIVE
30% of what we see	Looking at pictures	
20% of what we hear	Hearing words	
10% of what we read	Reading	

18

Where Should We Start?

Forming a good corporate culture starts at the top. An organization's culture reflects the style of the leader at the top, who casts a shadow on the next level of senior leader, who in turn casts a similar shadow onto their direct reports, and so on. Those who resist either get isolated or leave the organization, and what is left is a simple reflection of norms, habits, methods, and traits of those leaders. In some rare cases, organizations react against their leader and develop a culture opposite of the top leader's style. Eventually, that leader either leaves or is forced to leave because they're not a good culture fit.

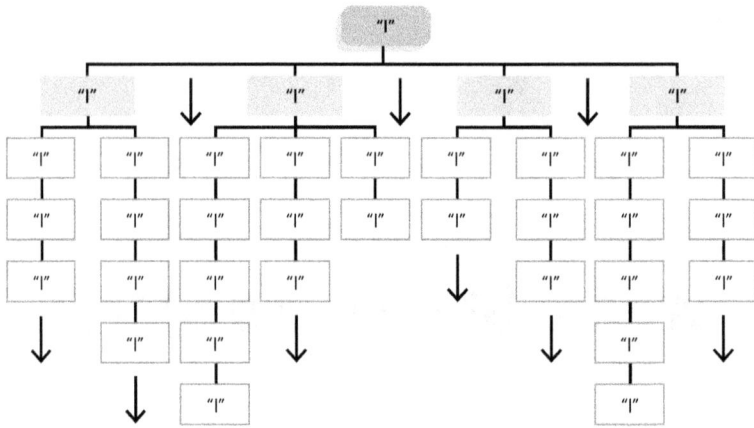

Larry Senn (senndelaney.com), the pioneer of corporate culture, refers to this as the "Shadow of the Leader," which cascades down to every level under. I like to call it the "Halo of the Leader" because the leader not only impacts employees below them but also peers, superiors, and everybody around.

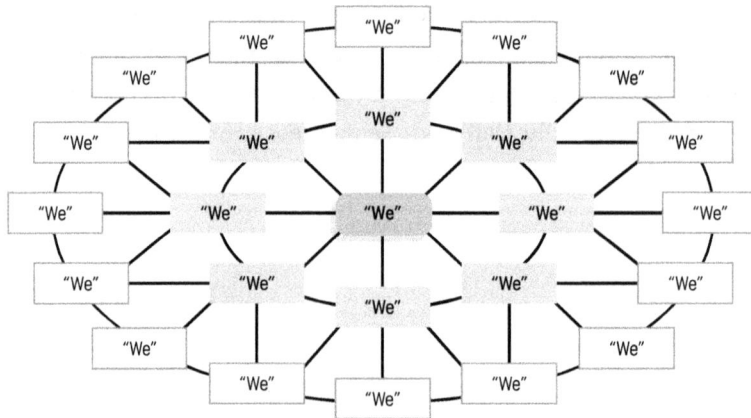

Many optimization and transformation initiatives fail to deliver their objectives because companies focus too much on the finish line instead of on building employees' capabilities. Building capabilities within organizations requires the coordination between departments that have such capabilities. For example, changes may be associated with technology, so the IT department should be engaged to help design and build training programs to allow employees to utilize new tech with proficiency. When operational capabilities require enhancement, such as learning and applying new processes, the operation department must be ready to sponsor those activities. Depending on the scale and size of the change, there are times when a dedicated person, department, or even specialized consulting agencies get involved to guide the development of the capabilities necessary for the business' success.

The following are a few logical steps related to where that work should start and how:

- Understand what new capabilities are vital to success based on the new objectives, processes, and tools.

- Diagnose the current capabilities by assessing the current state to understand if there are gaps between people's current capabilities and where they should be to function in the new environment.

- Design a future state and each capability by when it needs to be used and mastered.

- Align with leaders from different functions on the process, engagement needed, and approach.

- Build and deliver the capabilities by deploying learning, practicing, doing, and applying the new knowledge at work to reach the ability phase.

- Set up KPIs to measure the results.

- Adjust the strategies and tactics accordingly to focus on certain required capabilities that are more difficult to build.

- Establish a continuous improvement model to update skills and ensure that those capabilities stick.

19

Whom Should We Engage?

Business optimization and transformation requires a special type of leadership. As highlighted in chapters 12 and 17, good leaders not only have strategic vision, but they also encourage, inspire, and motivate employees to think outside of the box, innovate, and be positive disrupters in order to help their companies reshape their future and grow or transform to become safer, better, faster, and more profitable.

In addition, leaders should ensure a good, ethical workspace and stand for what is right no matter what. The positive culture that leaders build is critical to the success of the initiatives and the company. Positive culture promotes trust, passion, rapport, growth, compliance, ethics, authenticity, communication, and results.

THE PROJECT TEAM

The project team may be formed by people from the same department, different functions, separate entities, different countries, or even different companies. Team collaboration is key to creating a high-performing culture that is poised to meet the company's objectives.

The following elements are what usually create a great team that is positioned for success in almost any engagement.

A clear scope of work (SOW) needed: Once the project objectives are defined and communicated, the team can align their efforts on achieving those goals. As outlined in chapter 14, goals should always be SMART: specific, measurable, achievable, realistic and relevant, and timely. Business and project leaders should work on finalizing the goals and clearly communicating them to the team. The team should focus their efforts on the goals while aligning their own individual objectives with where the company is going.

A strong and inspiring leader: Business transformation or optimization efforts need a strong leader who can inspire people and get things done. A good leader is able to develop, support, engage, motivate, and empower team members in order to deliver the business objectives. Bill Gates once said: "As we look ahead into the next century, leaders will be those who empower others."[19] True leaders emerge when the business or initiative faces difficulties and the team members look to them for direction and support to remove impediments so they can keep moving forward with their work. One of the most crucial traits of a leader, especially when faced with problems, is the ability to facilitate and make effective decisions. The list of things that make an effective leader includes managing conflict, celebrating success, delegating responsibilities, trusting the team, and effectively communicating with all stakeholders.

An understanding of roles and responsibilities: Guessing what each employee is doing, stepping on each other's toes, duplicating work, and creating unnecessary friction among themselves because roles, responsibilities, and job descriptions have not been clearly defined are among the worst experiences a team can have. Leaders can avoid these conflicts by defining and communicating agreed-upon roles and responsibilities to help increase collaboration and transparency. A project management tool called RASCI can aid in the documentation and clarification of who is doing what during the execution of a project:

- **R (Responsible):** The person is responsible for doing the work and is supposed to make every effort to own the tasks at hand.

- **A (Accountable):** The person is accountable for the work being done and is liable for the outcomes, though they may or may not be the person actually doing the work.

- **S (Supportive):** The person actively supports the work and provides regular input to help the responsible.

- **C (Consulted):** The person offers occasional consultation when needed.

- **I (Informed):** This person is informed but does not necessarily take action unless asked to engage.

The right skills and experience: For teams to be successful, they need the right amount of knowledge and experience in the business areas that are being addressed. Different team members may have different personal and professional backgrounds; ideally, for a team to be able to accomplish the tasks assigned to them, their background experiences should complement and complete each other. Showing credibility and confidence in the work is also vital to earning the leadership's and teammates' trust. Some team members may need catching up, which can be addressed by the team leader and other members, whose job it is to support and rally each member to deliver the objectives. It may also be discovered that people on the team do not possess the right skills or character for the team or organization. In this case, management can try to help bring those members up to speed, but if that does not work, it is better to assign them to a different project and move on. It's best that the organization and team are not slowed down or derailed by one or more resources that may not be a good fit for the work at hand.

Clear and open communication: Effective communication is probably the most important characteristic of high-performing teams. Many issues can be reduced or even avoided through good communication upward, downward, and parallel. Listening to and respecting each other's opinion is one of the key factors in instilling trust and confidence. Also, effective communication reduces ambiguity and clarifies points, tasks, and objectives while allowing people to present ideas and opinions. Regular touch points are important throughout any project and can be accomplished via conference calls, meetings, emails, one-on-one sessions, reporting, and town halls. Encouraging each team member to have a voice and collaborate is also very important. Some people may be overpowered by position hierarchy or by dominant personnel in meetings or calls. It is the job of a strong and confident leader to open the space for all team members so they can confidently communicate and voice their opinions.

A positive and supportive atmosphere: Positivity is contagious. When team members are inspired and motivated to do a job, and when they know they are appreciated and supported, they will give their best to get the job done. An environment that is professional and open creates a sense of trust and safety among the team. People should also be able to have fun while they work efficiently to deliver objectives. On the other hand, a toxic environment limits creativity and discourages people from taking risks, for fear of punishment or judgment. A good working environment allows team members to establish professional relationships with each other based on respect and trust.

Diversity: Often a very understated factor in building effective teams, diversity is an extremely important practice that adds tremendous benefit to the team and organization. Diversity in the workplace means a representation of differences in gender, racial and ethnic background, sex, age, cultural background, religion, nationality, sexual orientation, color, accent, or skill, as well as those with disabilities. A diverse work environment provides a sense of comfort and belonging among different people. In fact, diversity enables broader perspectives, a great variety of lenses through which to view risks and issues, a wider range of skills, and a glut of original ideas that can add tremendous value to an organization.

Commitment: Effective teams are resilient and committed to achieving goals. They are highly energized and go above and beyond to get the job done. When team members feel they are in a self-driven and very focused work environment, they tend to ride those waves and mirror the team's spirit. Issues and hurdles should not cause teams to give up easily. A true leader helps keep the team inspired, motivated, and committed. At the same time, team members are the ones driving results, staying focused, and pushing till the business or project meets the objectives. When team members show true commitment to reaching set goals, their productivity and effectiveness peak, and eventually, the business objectives are met.

- A clear scope of work
- A strong and inspiring leader
- An understanding of roles and responsibilities
- The right skills and experience
- Clear and open communication
- A positive and supportive atmosphere
- Diversity
- Commitment

MANAGING RESISTANCE

When business leaders try to think differently to find opportunities, add value, innovate, and explore new business dimensions, they tend to change processes, technologies, and/or people's behavior. With any action, there is a reaction; the natural response to change is resistance. Change is not easy and can cause uncertainty and fear of the unknown. People usually prefer to deal with the devil they know! They realize it may not be good, but at least they can predict the outcomes.

Resistance may come from the project team members themselves, customers, workers, operators, or any other stakeholders. Generally speaking, roughly 5 to 15 percent of the general population of people exposed to change support it, 5 to 15 percent are usually against it, and the majority of the population are uncertain or unsure of their position.

Managing resistance is critical for the success of any business initiative. Business and project leaders should be skilled in finding the root cause of the resistance, understanding why people are resisting, and addressing fear by clearing ambiguities, communicating differences between the current and future states, and outlining steps and actions to be taken to make the change easier and more acceptable.

The objective here is to get everyone to embrace the proposed change and look forward to the outcome. The most successful tactic is to spend little time with the 5 to 15 percent of people who support change, because they will always support and look for transformation. They are not the challenge. Leaders should also limit time with those who represent the 5 to 15 percent of the population who are against change, because it is wasted energy trying to convince this group that change is good. To be successful in getting everyone on board, business leaders should focus their energy on the biggest population, the 70 to 90 percent, which is those who are uncertain about the changes to be made. If these people can be convinced to rally with the supporters, the majority of people would embrace and welcome change. In the end, the smaller population, the ones against change, would eventually follow the rest of the population who are supporting the change, or they would simply leave.

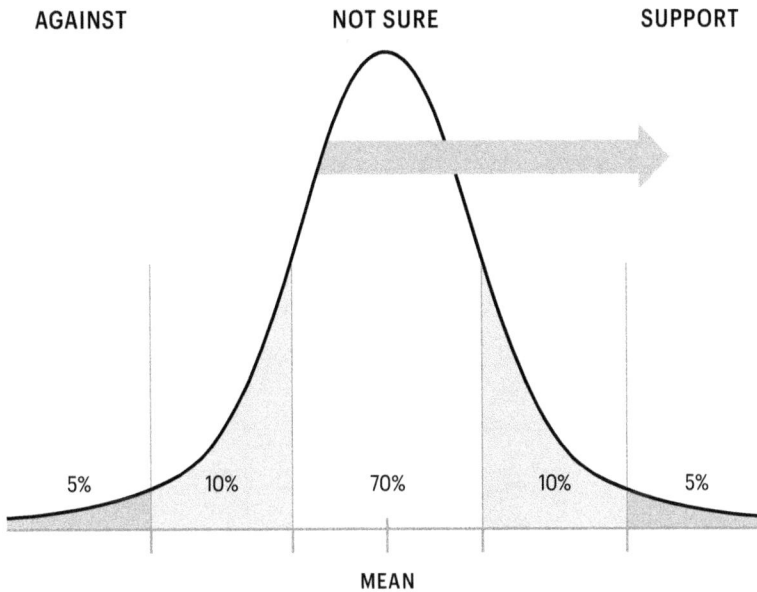

AGAINST	NOT SURE	SUPPORT

| 5% | 10% | 70% | 10% | 5% |

MEAN

Similarly, most politicians look for the majority of the votes by focusing on the middle, undecided population and trying to bring them to their cause. Time and money may be wasted focusing on the smaller population that may never change their minds, or on the other smaller population that have already made the decision to support the party or candidate.

20

When Do We Start to Perform?

As the team begins to engage in projects or initiatives, they tend to go through five sequential stages as described by Bruce Tuckman: Forming, Storming, Norming, Performing, Adjourning:[20]

- **Forming:** When a project starts, team members are usually anxious and have many questions about the project, the backgrounds of the people they first meet and are required to work with, and, of course, the leader. At this stage, they endeavor to keep calm while trying to figure out all the answers to their questions. Team members try not to pass judgment on a project or its people until they find out what is going on and who is doing what. Because the roles and responsibilities and project road maps may not be very clear at the beginning, the leader offers reassurance and remains confident in showing that these elements are being worked on and the project plan is going to clarify the scope and timelines.

- **Storming:** At this stage, people may start to clash due to continuing unclear roles and responsibilities or simply because of different backgrounds, personalities, or working styles. Frustration may start to become apparent. Some people may start to push for more authority or mark their territories. Maybe they start to get sensitive to the fact that the workload is not balanced, and some are working harder than others. Or, they could be uncomfortable with the approach the leader is taking in the project. While some of those issues can be expected and fixed by a strong and confident leader, other issues may linger and cause irreparable conditions such that team members leave voluntarily or involuntarily. A good leader quickly provides answers while helping the team stick to the goals and not become engaged in work politics. The leader may also establish regular one-on-one meetings or team meetings to get the team talking and expressing concerns as soon as they surface. Team-building exercises, lunches, dinners, or even happy hour gatherings can be very effective in bonding a team at this stage.

- **Norming:** With good leadership and a target-oriented mindset, the group starts to gradually move onto the norming phase, where they start to know and accept each other, think like a team, trust their leader, resolve their differences, and show appreciation for each other's skillsets. Sometimes a team will revert back to the storming phase, especially when they come across a new challenge, but when positively communicating with each other and with the support of a good leader, they come back to the norming stage and become stronger than ever.

- **Performing:** This stage is when the team members perform at their best and deliver great outcomes. They communicate together, clearing hurdles that cause friction while aiming for the project's ultimate goal. The continuous support and inspiration from the leader are critical in sustaining that energy and maintaining a trusting environment among the team with a focus on delivering the objectives and realizing rewards.

- **Adjourning:** As indicated in earlier chapters, a project usually has a beginning and an end. Some or all members of the team usually go back to their day job, find new opportunities, engage in other projects, or continue on different paths within the program at hand. In other words, the project team members adjourn to do other things. At this stage, the leader acknowledges and rewards the team for a job well done if the project reached the finish line as required and within its budget and time. Or, if the project did not meet some or all of its objectives, the leader works on a postmortem to document areas to be handled better in the future.

PEOPLE FACE REALITY, THEN GENERALLY ACCEPT AND MOVE ON

People tend to get anxious and worried when they are impacted by change in their workspace, the way they do their job, or the hierarchy of people with whom they work. Depending on the significance and impact of the change on a person's life, they may go through similar stages to those seen when someone faces grief or loss, though perhaps to a lesser degree. In her best-selling book *On Death and Dying* (1969), well-known psychiatrist Elisabeth Kübler-Ross outlined the five stages of grief (otherwise known as the Kübler-Ross model) that people usually experience emotionally when they have lost loved ones:

1. Denial: People's first reaction when they learn about a significant negative change in their life is to deny the reality of the situation. Emotions rush in quickly and they become confused, then defensive, and make statements such as, "This cannot be happening; this is not true; there must be something to change it back!" The shock of loss and change limits their ability to accept the facts. Typically, people try to isolate themselves and often think things will never be good again after such a life-changing event. In this stage of employee mentality, a good business leader explains the reasons for change and the long-term ramifications of not making the changes. They comfort employees but avoid placating them. A good leader remains strong, aspirational, and optimistic in order to help upset employees move from this stage as quickly as possible.

2. Anger: The next stage people experience is anger as they realize how helpless and vulnerable they feel. They begin to realize that what has happened or is happening is real, and that things will impact them and their lives one way or another. Intense emotion usually accompanies this stage, and they may express this emotion by breaking things, cursing, and shouting at people around them. Questions arise, such as, "Why me?" Common statements are, "This is ridiculous, I cannot live like this!" Adding fuel to the fire at this stage is the worst thing a business leader can do. A good leader should try to absorb some of the anger, focus on positivity, and express confidence in the future. Some people may get too emotional and lose focus at this stage, and cause intentional or unintentional harm to themselves or their organization.

3. Bargaining: As people calm down after the shock of change or loss, they try to regain control of the situation by bargaining. They start to realize that there is probably nothing they can do to change what has happened and reduce the emotional pain they feel. Feeling a lack of control, people sometimes try to blame themselves, and look to a higher power to alter the situation. Statements that come out during this stage include, "If only I could change the past! I promise I will change or do things differently if I can go back in time! God, I will forever be a good person if you fix this issue." Business leaders may want to emphasize the fact that the new reality will likely not revert to a prior state. They should provide employees with resources to support them emotionally if needed. Many companies hire a therapist or dedicate members of their teams to offer support and give comfort. They can also provide an anonymous toll-free number to offer support and personal consultation during this stage.

4. Depression: At this stage, people realize that anger and bargaining are not working so they start to pull inward. Regret, sadness, and isolation become the dominant feelings. People enter a depressive state that can linger based on the depth of the change or loss. Business leaders can help ease the depression by offering reassurance and support, and continue to provide therapy resources and personal consultation to help their employees out of their depressive state.

5. Acceptance: While this may not be a period of happiness, at this stage, people no longer resist the reality of the situation. Sadness and regret sometimes continue to be present, but there is much less denial, anger, bargaining, and depression. At this point, people start to realize that the change or loss they're experiencing is just a part of life and they have to live with it. In fact, with proper support and encouragement from others around, including business leaders, they may start to find a bright side to what has happened. In many cases, people's work performance begins to regain its prior momentum.

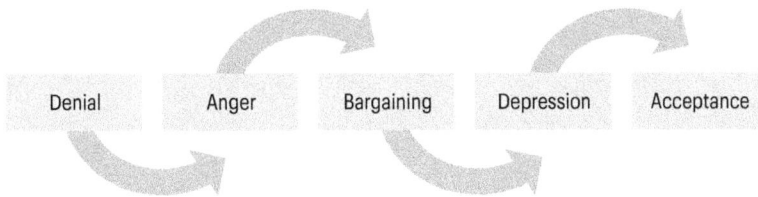

| Denial | Anger | Bargaining | Depression | Acceptance |

21

How Should We Work Together?

A corporate culture is the personality of a company. The policies, benefits, communication, experiences, interactions between employees, and interactions with customers are some elements that define the culture. Many companies nowadays are establishing metrics and KPIs to regularly measure cultural impact in the workplace. This is particularity important because a positive culture is the foundation of a successful organization. It also promotes trust, collaboration, and respect while motivating people and inspiring them to take care of the business and its customers.

Among these measures are:

- **Recruiting processes and turnaround time:** How many days does it take to approve, post, interview, and fill a position?

- **Placement experience:** How do candidates view the hiring experience (process, communication, background check, etc.)?

- **Rate of job satisfaction:** Are employees satisfied at work? How do they view their leader? How do they view work–life balance?

- **Loyalty:** Would employees stay with the company if they were offered a similar or slightly better job at another company?

- **Collaboration:** Collaboration can lead to amazing results. Therefore, companies strive to increase collaboration and measure its effectiveness. Questions usually asked are: Is teamwork part of the everyday work environment? Is communication open and effective? Are social interaction and inclusiveness part of the culture?

- **Equality:** No person should experience or fear discrimination anywhere, and especially in the workplace. Corporations establish surveys and direct lines to measure equality in the workplace and avoid discrimination based on disabilities and differences in gender, race, sex, age, cultural background, religion, nationality, sexual orientation, color, or even accent.

- **Performance rating:** Quarterly, semiannual, or even annual reviews are part of many companies' culture so that employees' performances can be measured. Rewards, bonuses, and promotions should be offered based on facts. Communication is encouraged between employees and managers to allow for frequent coaching and constructive feedback when necessary.

- **Stress level:** Stressed employees are less productive than those who are not. Stress is easily transferred to customers who interact with stressed employees. Companies nowadays measure employee stress levels to understand if there is too much work on their plates such that it cannot be achieved, or if there are issues that are causing anxiety and unrest among the workforce.

- **Wellness programs:** A healthy body usually facilitates a healthy mind. Many companies hire specialists and establish clinics to build a wellness program to measure employee health and provide services to address health issues. Preventive health practices not only allow employees to be on the job consistently, but also save companies money as a result of fewer insurance claims and avoiding spiking insurance rates. Annual or semiannual health checks are encouraged, while company-subsidized or discounted memberships at sports centers are becoming the norm to encourage a healthy lifestyle.

- **Social responsibility:** It is everyone's duty to protect society and the environment. This topic has become increasingly important to companies and individuals. Employees these days are proud to work for companies that promote social responsibility such as donating to charities, sponsoring charitable events, investing in lowering their carbon footprint, minimizing waste, and becoming energy-efficient.

- **Employee turnover rate (ETR):** Recruiting, hiring, and relocating employees is quite costly. Therefore, companies should establish measures to monitor the number of people who are voluntarily or involuntarily leaving them. In a growing economy, there is often much competition for good employees; otherwise, this exercise helps identify problems within a department or the entire company that can be addressed by leaders in order to achieve and maintain employee retention.

- **Net promoter score (NPS):** This indicator is usually collected through annual surveys that measure customer and employee satisfaction and loyalty. It is geared toward understanding how likely customers and employees are to suggest and recommend the business to friends or family both for sales and work opportunities. The survey usually asks several questions about the experiences dealing with or working in the company. Survey results can be analyzed and quantified in an index ranging from -100 to +100.

SIGNS OF A POSITIVE CULTURE

When a healthy, positive culture is realized, the organization and its leaders can enjoy the fruition of the hard work that made it possible. The following are signs that can easily be seen or felt in companies that have such a culture:

- **Successful, profitable, and sustainable business:** Healthy cultures and good, profitable bottom lines are positively correlated. It is no secret that the most successful companies in any industry typically enjoy a positive culture that is felt across all levels in the organization and reflected through customer experience.

- **Team spirit:** Businesses depends on teams, as everyone in the organization needs someone else's help in some shape or form. Companies with a good and healthy culture that encourages open communication and frequent interaction among employees enjoy a team-oriented atmosphere.

- **Effective leadership:** Effective leadership positively correlates with great organizational cultures. Leadership styles can reinforce values and push toward growing profitable businesses while at the same time inspiring people and holding them accountable to deliver those outcomes.

- **Work–life balance:** When employees are overloaded with work and stressed, their performance, health, and loyalty to the company suffer. There are many benefits to finding the right work–life balance by providing means of flexibility and ensuring that employees take adequate vacation time. A healthy culture is visible when employees realize that they are not frequently overstretched and overworked.

- **Smiles and a pleasant attitude:** Probably one of the most obvious things that can be seen and felt as soon as someone enters a company is the outward disposition of company staff toward others. This includes the way customers, suppliers, or couriers are greeted at the door or over the phone, or the tone in emails and during meetings or even when bumping into a coworker in the elevator or hallways. Smiles, good posture, pleasant greetings, and laughter among employees all reflect a positive company culture.

- **Low employee turnover:** In today's business environment, employees often prefer to stay with companies that provide better working conditions than those that pay slightly more or offer a better title. If employees are satisfied where they are, they are unlikely to leave their employer. They are normally happy as long as their company appreciates their efforts, pays them competitively, and offers them a positive working environment. It is not a stretch to assume that companies with high employee turnover have a suboptimal corporate culture.

- **Energy:** When there are obvious signs of energy, engagement, and motivation among employees, there is definitely a positive and healthy culture in place. When employees feel that the company's business is like their own, they give it 110 percent to ensure its success. This energy is similar to entrepreneurs who feel the motivation and desire to build and grow their own business every day.

- **Job security:** Happy employees are usually not afraid to lose their job, because they trust the organization, its leaders, and the business model. A good corporate culture is obvious when employees are confident and have a sense of job security. Those employees are not worried that the company will lose its business or that they will lose their job. They come to work every day with full energy focused on doing their job and not wasting time searching for alternative opportunities.

- **Open communication:** A healthy, positive workplace culture is apparent when leaders and employees, and employees among themselves, communicate with each other in a clear and collaborative way. Transparent and open communication removes the tendency toward employee gossip, assumptions, or backstabbing. It also inspires confidence and trust that there will not be any radical shifts in direction without proper communication and feedback openness.

THE ART AND SCIENCE OF TRAINING EMPLOYEES

Organizations ideally welcome employees from different professional and educational backgrounds. Essentially, they put training programs in place to help new employees get up to speed and learn the company's way of doing things, and to allow them to perform their jobs efficiently and well. Business leaders should also encourage constant improvement, and reward those people who can bring ideas to the table that enable the company to do the job safer, better, faster, and maybe cheaper.

Employees' capabilities can be enhanced and developed through training, coaching, job shadowing, practices, and continued education. However, most of the time, business leaders focus too much on the "what" aspect and forget the "how" elements. Getting a job done is both a science and an art—a science based on processes and tools, and also the art of dealing with people effectively. In other words, employees are usually given tools and shown the techniques to use them, but many have no coaching as to how they can control their emotions and use certain techniques to better communicate and behave effectively. Leaders often fail to realize the importance of developing certain skills such as how to communicate and work with people, because generally those topics are not taught well during the years of formal education or in business schools.

Emotional Intelligence

This is also referred to as the emotional quotient (EQ). Whereas the intelligence quotient (IQ) measures intelligence through a test that typically scores how smart an individual is, considering that person's age and abilities such as memory, quantitative reasoning, knowledge, and visual and spatial processing, the EQ measures the person's ability to recognize their own emotions, control their behavior, and understand how their emotions and behavior can impact others in a positive way, whether in getting a point across, effectively communicating and convincing, empathizing, or resolving conflicts and challenges. Writers such as well-known psychologist

Daniel Goleman (author of international best seller *Emotional Intelligence: Why It Can Matter More Than* IQ, among others) have long been shedding light on the importance of emotional intelligence.

Emotional intelligence helps people identify emotions, control feelings, perceive others' points of view, build relationships, and succeed in life whether at home, school, or work. EQ can also help turn negative energy into positive energy and less optimal intention into constructive action that benefits the individual and their organization.

Emotional intelligence can be defined by the following attributes:

- **Self-awareness:** A person's level of self-awareness is evident by how well they recognize their emotions and the effect of those emotions on their thoughts and behavior. A well-developed sense of self also allows a person to honestly see and evaluate their own strengths and weaknesses. Conversely, others have an unclear vision of who they really are and how they behave; some see themselves as they wish to be seen, such as highly competent or understanding and empathetic, but this image of themselves may be far from the truth. Successful people often ask those around them for feedback on what they are doing and how they can be better. Being open to feedback, even if it is sometimes negative, is the first step toward raising self-awareness. Acknowledging the possible truth of negative feedback and overcoming the often immediate internal denial, is the next step. Practicing humility, paying attention to one's own feelings, and even meditating in an effort to become more self-aware are ways to help people realize they are not perfect—there are always areas to develop and opportunities to learn from mistakes.

- **Self-management:** People need to be able to control their impulsive feelings and behaviors at work, particularly when things do not go as planned or desired. Panicking or exploding in anger, for example, can bring down the workspace by disrupting momentum, positive energy, and morale. Managing emotions in a healthy and calm way, with the mindset of adapting to changing circumstances and putting actions in place to address the situation, is the smartest way to respond. Those who are self-managed or self-regulated are almost always able to avoid attacking others verbally or physically, or rushing into a regrettable decision that compromises their reputation. Good leaders often remind themselves of their responsibilities and practice staying calm under stress. Some tactics of self-management during conflict are pausing to breathe deeply, walking around or getting some fresh air to clear the mind, writing down emotions in a journal, and avoiding sending any potentially inflammatory emails until the next day when emotions are not so high.

- **Self-motivation:** High energy, persistence, and self-motivation are key success factors for anybody. Employees who are unhappy about their job or who cannot find purpose in their work typically drag their feet to do it, and the quality of their work is often mediocre. A high-energy leader or staff member can reflect their energy to the individuals around them. Self-motivation drives individuals to keep going, face difficulties or setbacks, find resolution, discover opportunities, and always commit to achieving their goals. Being self-motivated is usually dependent on people's purpose in life, goals, and priorities. So, for those people who are not self-motivated, it can help to reflect on who they really are, what value they can add, what exactly they want to do in life, what truly motivates them, and how to adopt an optimistic mindset. Other tactics to help with self-motivation are surrounding oneself with good, high-energy people, putting actions in place, and tracking one's own progress with a confident outlook.

- **Empathy and social skills:** Successful people know how to build relationships and understand others' emotions, needs, and concerns. They are able to establish and maintain positive relationships because they believe in the power of "we," not "I." Those who can look at situations from other people's perspectives usually gain the trust, confidence, and appreciation of those around them because they are able to listen and genuinely offer help. Leaders are especially effective when they practice good social skills and show empathy toward their employees and peers. Leaders such as these are usually the most respected, supported, and successful in their companies.

Communication, Communication, Communication

To be both personally and professionally successful, one of the most important life skills to have is the ability to effectively communicate with people. Many people spend over 80 percent of their day communicating, yet this skill receives very little attention at schools or work. Interestingly, because people communicate all the time, they often assume they are communicating well with everyone around them. For communication to be effective, however, the sender needs to ensure that the intended message has been delivered and understood clearly by the receiver. The fact is that many times, while people assume this has been accomplished, the receiver on the other side of the communication channel has no idea of the true message, or they have interpreted it in their own way.

Some are naturally gifted as good communicators, but savvy communicators develop the skills through training, practice, and listening to feedback.

Communication is not only verbal. Body language or tone can totally change the meaning of a message. What follows are components of communication.

Verbal: As humans grow up, interact with each other, go to schools, enter the workforce, listen to news, watch movies, and so on, they tend to develop their own method of using verbal cues to structure their communication style. Savvy communicators avoid the use of potentially inflammatory "danger" phrases and replace them with "power" phrases. Here are examples of danger phrases to avoid and what power phrases to use instead, especially in business:

☒ Avoid saying: "I disagree."
☑ Replace with: "I see it differently."

☒ Avoid saying: "We need to talk!"
☑ Replace with: "I need your help!"

☒ Avoid saying: "What's wrong with you?"
☑ Replace with: "What's bothering you?"

☒ Avoid saying: "I need the assignment by…"
☑ Replace with: "The assignment is due by…"

☒ Avoid saying: "Do you need…?"
☑ Replace with: "Would you like to…?"

☒ Avoid saying: "What were you thinking?"
☑ Replace with: "In the future, when you come across something like this, I suggest you do the following… because…"

☒ Avoid saying: "I am sorry for…"
☑ Replace with: "Apologies for…"

☑ Always start with thank you or other words of appreciation, and end with thank you.

Visual: A picture can really say a thousand words. Visual communication can comprise images, art, acts, signs, gestures, body language, and video clips. Combining visual and verbal communication techniques can be very powerful. This is truly an art and requires much practice, especially body language and gestures. It is very important to note that people should be extremely careful when working with others from different cultures or countries because gestures and body language can mean totally different things from one culture to another. For example, in American and European cultures, tilting the head sideways means that a person is unsure or does not fully agree, but in Indian culture, it can mean that the person is in agreement or understands what is being said. Also, while a communicator (sender) may have good intentions, the receiver may view what they convey as an insult. For example, Americans often show their approval or satisfaction with the OK hand signal, which in the Arabic culture means that the person is coming forward to fight; that gesture is also considered rude in Brazil. Whereas "thumbs-up" is considered positive in many countries, in Bangladesh, it is an insult. And while crossing our fingers in North America is a wish for good luck, in Vietnam, it symbolizes female genitalia.

Below are some examples of common body language or gestures that can significantly change the meaning of verbal cues in Western society:

- Side head tilt (passive) versus forward head tilt (assertive): Think about how dogs communicate aggression by forward-tilting their head, while on the other hand tilting their head to the side to show compassion. Same principle with human beings.

- Shoulder-to-shoulder sidle up (relaxed) versus head-on (aggressive). Similar to the previous dog example, when dogs want to fight, they move head-on in a straight line, while when they like each other, they circle around each other side-to-side or shoulder-to-shoulder.

- The three-second look: If someone wants to show another that they really mean what they say and want to strongly emphasize a point, they give the other person a three-second stare. Note that if it is less than that, it is not enough to show how serious the person is, and if it is more than that, it is disrespectful and shows unprofessionalism.

- Mirroring: This is an extremely powerful technique to master in order to obtain acceptance. People generally become comfortable with people who are like them, share a similar background, or speak in the same way. Mirroring means that the person tries to copy the other person's body language like a mirror to gain comfort and acceptance. People need to be careful not to go too far and mimic everything the other person does, which typically backfires and demonstrates disrespect and immaturity.

- Eye contact: Eye contact is essential to grabbing attention and displaying or giving one confidence. If one person is talking while the other is looking elsewhere, chances are that the person looking away is not following the conversation and does not care about what is being communicated. Savvy communicators ensure they make eye contact with their audience.

- Crossed arms: Unless someone is feeling very cold, they should try to avoid crossing their arms in meetings or when talking to others. Crossed arms typically means that the person is being defensive or close-minded while not feel very good about a situation. Although it may be comfortable, it is definitely not advisable to cross arms unless the message is meant to actually show disagreement or a lack of cooperation.

- Physical barriers: Another good technique to practice especially during meetings or interviews is removing physical barriers between communicators. Items as simple as a computer, furniture, coffee cups, a tissue box, or a phone are physical barriers that can also create an emotional barrier. Removing these would demonstrate a clear and open environment between communicators.

- Owning the room: It is amazing how many people sit in meetings, especially with more important people, and become reserved or withdrawn. They tend to keep their arms tight to their body, pull their personal items close to them, and lower their heads slightly. A question I usually ask those people is: "Do you sit like this at home and at your dinner table?" Why not feel at home! Confidence inspires trust, so spread your wings and show that you belong here too.

Vocal: This means the tone of voice and volume used during communication. If a voice is pleasant and authoritative, it will inspire confidence. People may need to adapt their tone to the topic, situation, and surroundings. The following are some examples of vocal elements of communication:

- Volume: If the room is small and quiet and there are only a few people, it is best for the speaker to lower their voice somewhat and speak softly so they are not too loud and don't make the audience uncomfortable. On the other hand, if the room is noisy or if the speakers are not using a microphone in a large room, then they should raise their voice to be heard clearly and understood.

- Tone quality: Probably the worst type of communicator is one who speaks in monotone. Even if the content of their presentation is excellent and full of useful information, if a speaker does not know how to deliver the message in an engaging tone, they will be ineffective. After a short period of time, the communicator will begin to lose the audience's attention. A good way to be an effective communicator is to use vocal inflection during a speech or presentation to draw attention to vital information and maintain people's interest.

- Pace or speed: Savvy communicators know how to speak with a good pace to allow people to receive and understand their content without boring them. Finding that right speed is important in order to keep the audience engaged. Some people are anxious and just want to finish their presentation or speech quickly. This can cause information to be lost or unclear. On the other hand, speaking too slowly can cause boredom.

- Breath: It is totally fine to pause while communicating. In fact, it is advisable. Not only does it provide the audience the chance to digest the message, but it also allows the speaker to breathe and get oxygen to fuel the brain, ensures constant focus, and is effective in better illustrating points. Pausing a little also gives the speaker time to regather their thoughts if necessary and ready themselves for the next topic.

• Avoidance of "crutch words": There is probably nothing more annoying than hearing a speaker often repeat certain words during a conversation or presentation. Those speakers may not even know they are doing it and often deny it is happening until someone shows them a recording. Repeating words like "um," "uhhh," and "you know" can quickly cause the audience to lose patience and focus.

Listening: Yes, one communication skill is listening—and not only hearing. Hearing is merely the physiological process of sounds reaching the ears, while listening requires that the receivers make efforts to decode, understand, and interpret messages from the sender. Communication can be easily misinterpreted when people do not effectively listen to each other. When those speaking realize their audience is not listening, they typically become frustrated and lose control. Communicators should ensure that they grab and keep the attention of their listeners, and that their topics are informative and relevant. Listeners should avoid distractions and make an effort to focus on the material being presented. In today's advanced technology environment, people are distracted very easily by emails, social media, marketing offers, and whatever messages or notifications they get on their phones. A good practice is for all people in the room to turn off their phones or put them on "do not disturb" mode to allow them to focus on what is being communicated.

Written: All businesses rely on written communication between their employees, leaders, owners, suppliers, and customers. Written messages can be transferred via emails, reports, letters, memos, presentations, newsletters, instant messaging, billboards, and so on. Some people are more effective than others at writing, and that is natural. But there are some key items that should be pointed at in order to make any person a better communicator. Things like:

- Beginning with a greeting
- Having a clear subject line
- Stating the purpose
- Clarifying the ask and list actions
- Writing closing remarks
- Running a spell check
- Avoiding emojis and playful colors and fonts, unless the message is intended to be very casual and fun

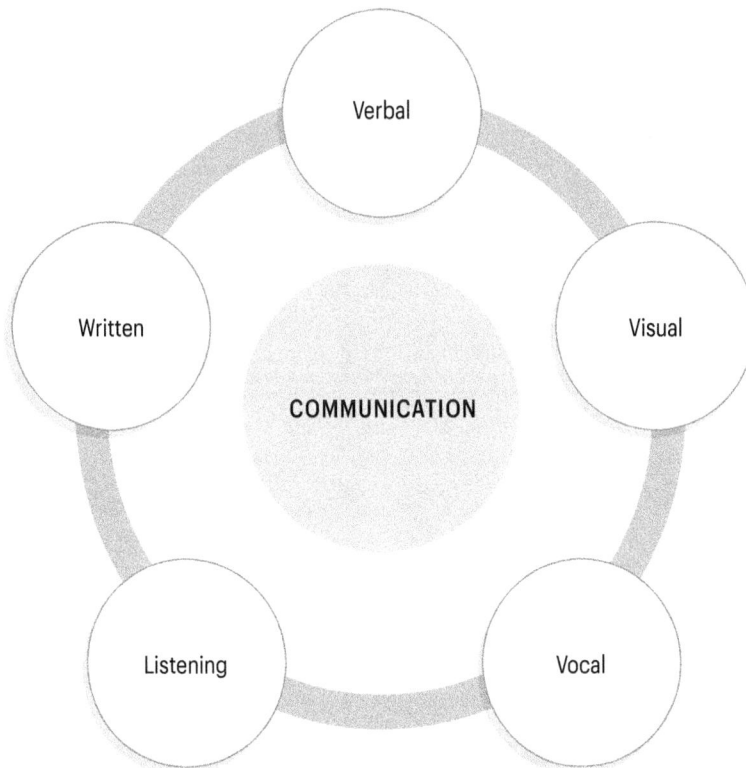

22

How Much Should We Invest in People?

Investing in employees is one of the smartest business decisions leaders can make. But why? The following are good reasons for companies to invest generously in people:

- **Competitive advantage:** It is extremely difficult for competitors to replicate great employee morale and company culture. The most successful businesses are those that have the best employees. An organization with a good reputation for employee satisfaction is able to attract and retain talent easier than their competitors and thus build their human assets.

- **Happier customers:** Richard Branson said, "Clients do not come first. Employees come first. If you take care of your employees, they will take care of the clients."[21] Many may argue against this idea, as customers ultimately are the ones who purchase the company's products or services. However, excellent, loyal employees take care of customers well, and those customers then become loyal themselves, which makes the business more profitable and able to sustain a competitive advantage while taking care of employees and stockholders.

- **Business growth:** Not only do happy employees take good care of customers, but they are also likely the ones who bring forward the best and most effective ideas to grow the business or save the company money. The brightest ideas usually come from employees, not business leaders.

- **Higher efficiency:** Efficiency is also always at its peak when employees are motivated and satisfied at work, because their productivity is usually very high. Employees who look forward to coming into work every day are likely to do a far better job than those who drag their feet to go to work.

- **Attract talent:** Happy employees are likely to be vocal about their good employers. They are likely to tell the people in their personal and professional networks about their experiences or even write about them online or on social media.

The following are some ideas to consider as part of investing in employees:

- Competitive paycheck
- Good benefits and health insurance
- More vacation days
- Flexible work hours
- Option to work remotely
- Paid training
- Increased engagement
- Opportunity to grow and get promoted
- Continued education reimbursement
- Professional development
- Extended paid parental leave
- Free or subsidized gym membership
- Assisted day care service
- Free or subsidized food
- Recognition and awards

Mutual respect between employer and employee is key to succeeding in today's business environment. The people companies hire and invest in can make or break their business. Investing in employees is a good use of money, time, and energy because that investment pays back, and in good return.

In Part Three, I addressed the "people" element of business, and why it is important to put a solid change management practice in place when making changes in an organization, especially during business optimization and transformation. I highlighted the importance of effective communication and a good corporate culture to allow employees to deliver the organization's objectives. In Part Four, I will present the importance of always being prepared for risk and having a contingency plan ready—because unexpected things happen and major events can present significant risk to an organization.

Why do things almost never go according to plan?

What just happened? Why are we facing
this crisis now?

How can we address catastrophic events?

Why were we hit harder than others?
Should we plan better next time?

How can we avoid catastrophic business consequences from risks and issues we are facing?

PART FOUR

READINESS FOR UNEXPECTED EVENTS

23

Risk, Crisis, and Contingency Plans

Catastrophic events can happen at any time, often without prior notice. All businesses are susceptible to crises, which is why it is important to have a contingency plan ready to avoid significant damage to the company or going out of business.

One example of such upheaval is the 2020 COVID-19 crisis, which not only forced the majority of our global population to stay home and practice physical distancing, but also took its toll on many businesses and did devastating damage to the health, wealth, and financial status of countless individuals.

HOW TO IDENTIFY RISKS AND ISSUES

Once a company establishes its plans to optimize or transform its business, it is critical that they put a mechanism in place to avoid potential failure points. To do that, there should be a process for identifying any potential risks that could happen and any issues at hand.

A risk is a potential event that has not happened yet and has a certain degree of probability to occur in the future. An issue is a risk that has happened. Here's how to identify risks and issues:

- **Historical data:** The first step in trying to identify risk is to look for data from prior projects and examine any postmortem documents from prior efforts. Presuming that documentation from past or similar engagements is clear and meaningful, the data can be very helpful in understanding what hurdles past teams encountered, how they addressed risks and issues, and what were the recommendations from prior teams to address similar problems. If historical data does not exist in the company, data can usually be purchased from agencies or consulting companies that have gone through similar journeys and have meticulously documented lessons learned.

- **Interviewing:** Providing that there is no confidentiality issue surrounding the transformational effort, meeting and interviewing employees from different functions and across several verticals could help in getting information about experiences they may have had in similar engagements during their tenure at the company or from experience at other organizations. Also, depending on the level of confidentiality and if nondisclosure agreements (NDAs) are in place, interviewing can be conducted with stakeholders from outside the company, such as suppliers and partners.

- **Brainstorming:** A group of stakeholders can be summoned to a brainstorming session to generate predictions of what could go wrong in the transformation effort.

- **Assumptions analysis:** This technique is similar to brainstorming, but it is done only with a limited group, and usually when there is no time for other techniques or when the endeavor is new to the world and there is no historical data or applicable experience. Sometimes this is called a premortem—a hypothetical scenario in which a team imagines that a transformational effort has failed and then works backward to determine what potentially could lead to that failure.

- **Transparent reporting and escalation:** As the team goes through the business transformation journey, they will likely encounter issues that could or could not have been identified before. A RAID log is advisable in this case, to document each of the risks and issues, as well as actions that can be taken in response either immediately or in the future. However, establishing a log is one thing, but keeping it active and visible is another. Stakeholders are usually busy doing their job, so reminding the project team of the issues and risks on a regular basis is important. At the same time, an escalation path of issues and risks should be established to quickly identify which should be handled immediately and by whom to avoid serious problems in the future.

It is very common to see team members talk about or exchange notes on risks and issues. However, they often fail to properly document or remind the stakeholders about them, or take proper action to address them. Therefore, it is important to maintain a log for risks and issues to document the problems, the dates they were logged, who is monitoring or taking action, the severity of the problems, and the expected dates by which the team believe a resolution or impact should be expected.

HOW TO RESPOND TO RISKS AND ISSUES

The response tactics to risks and issues should always be in the following order: Avoid, Mitigate, Transfer, Accelerate, Accept, and Escalate.

With every action, there are potential consequences. In other words, by tackling one risk, an organization could introduce new ones that are unplanned and unpredictable. Those new risks can be in two categories:

1. Secondary risks: A new risk created when responding to the initial risk. The team should have a plan to address those secondary risks as they appear.

2. Residual risks: A risk that remains even after responding to the initial risk. With a residual risk, there's usually not much one can do—it's here to stay.

Below, I outline risk response tactics with examples to help illustrate and clarify each element, as well as the secondary or residual risks that can surface as reactions to each response taken.

Avoid: Risk can sometimes be avoided by removing the cause or changing direction while still targeting to deliver the objectives. Of course, not all risks can be avoided, either partially or completely. Also, sometimes this tactic can cause delays, add cost, or even change the scope to accommodate risk avoidance especially if the risk is big.

For example, say someone is driving a vehicle on the highway at 65 miles per hour and they see a big pothole ahead. Their first tactic would be to look left and right, maintain speed, safely change lanes, avoid the pothole, then change back to the previous lane. In this case, the driver is then able to reach their destination with almost no impact to trip time or added cost. But suppose that the driver notices a huge avalanche on the horizon—now, their options are limited, and they may elect to avoid the road altogether and take a longer route, or even turn around and cancel the trip based on the seriousness of the road conditions and limited safe options.

A secondary risk could be missing the trip goals due to delays in the journey.

A residual risk would be the damage or accident the large pothole could still cause every time travelers took that road.

Mitigate: Risk mitigation means using tactics that can reduce the probability and/or severity of the impact in the event that a risk is unavoidable. The key to risk mitigation is early detection, so the risk is less severe. This type of response to risk can cause delays in execution, increase costs, and/or add resources.

In the driving example illustrated earlier, say the driver sees the big pothole ahead while two semitrucks are on either side preventing any lane change. The next best option, then, is to apply the brakes to lower the speed of the vehicle and reduce the severity of the impact of the pothole.

The secondary risk could be the destruction of any cargo in the vehicle due to the sudden reduction of speed.

The residual risk could be that while the vehicle does hit the pothole, despite hitting it at a lower speed, it suffers damage to the axle or tires that may not appear immediately.

Think about the *Titanic*. The captain tried to avoid the iceberg but could not, so he tried to lower the speed and steer away from it so as not to hit it head-on. Despite the fact that the *Titanic* did not hit the iceberg head-on or at full speed, the residual risk was that the impact caused the ship to sink because there was nothing that could have been done to address the consequences of the impact.

Transfer: Transferring risk means assigning the work to a third party who would assume the responsibilities and be accountable for any liabilities and risk. This can be used either when the other party knows how to handle the situation better or when an organization just wants to transfer the whole risk associated with a job and worry about other things that could be of more importance. Risk transfer almost always costs more money, so it would likely impact the budget.

In the driving example illustrated earlier, the driver may find that the road is very dangerous because of numerous potholes or avalanches and thus elects to hire a taxi, transferring the risk to the cab instead of causing damage to their car.

The secondary risk in this example could be that the taxi driver is not very experienced or may have had a few drinks before the journey, thus causing new risks, so the passenger should make sure that the taxi company is reputable and has good and responsible drivers.

The residual risk could be that while riding in the taxi, an accident happens due to potholes or avalanches, thereby harming both the taxi driver and passenger.

Accelerate: The risk acceleration strategy is usually used when there is an opportunity within a risk and the organization finds it beneficial to accelerate the risk event so that they can move ahead and focus on the targeted opportunities.

Risk acceleration can be realized through three tactics:

1. Exploit: The objective here is to add tasks or activities in order to ensure that the opportunity happens. The reason for the acceleration is to eliminate the risk of uncertainty and make sure the opportunity occurs quickly.

2. Enhance: This tactic aims at increasing the positive risk and amplifying the opportunities. The objective here is to maximize the benefits of this positive risk, fuel it, and ensure it happens.

3. Share: If the organization does not have the right resources to realize the potential benefits of the opportunity at hand, then it may hire another company that is specialized in addressing the risk and ensuring that the benefits are captured. This is very similar to the risk transfer of threats, but in this case, it is meant to have a positive impact, and the relationship with the third party here is a partnership to maximize the probability of the opportunity occurring and increase the potential benefits for both parties.

Suppose there is an uprising against or impeachment of a corrupt political leader. While this could cause numerous threats or risks of casualties, or a negative impact on the economy, there could also be opportunities for future growth if the corrupt leader is ousted. The resistance may exploit the opportunity by making sure they keep the pressure on and continuing to engage the people and media. The resistance may also enhance the risks to speed up the impeachment process and try to potentially reduce the number of casualties and degradation of the economy. They may increase the intensity of the impeachment activities, and try to force a power takeover by finding allies in government and the military to overthrow the corrupt leader. The resistance may not have the strength or funds to do all this, however, so they may partner with a foreign country that has the power and influence to help them, either by gathering worldwide support or even entering their country with military power under a certain agreement to share future benefits. This option often comes with long-term negative consequences (in this case, secondary risk), such as foreign invasion and control of natural resources or even the government.

Accept: If all options for risk avoidance, mitigation, transfer, or acceleration have been exploited, then there is no other recourse for an organization but to accept the risks and bear any impact they may cause. Basically, the Acceptance strategy is utilized when it is not possible or practical to address a risk by any other strategies.

There are two types of risk acceptance:

1. Active acceptance: This means that the organization is now aware of the risks and has or is preparing a contingency plan to be ready to address the consequences of the risks.

2. Passive acceptance: Simply put, this means "just do nothing." In this case, there are no feasible response options to address the risks, and the organization can just wait for those risks to happen.

Going back to the driving example, say the driver cannot avoid the pothole because of the two semitrucks on either side, and they are unable to reduce their speed to lower the impact because another vehicle is tailgating them. If the driver cannot transfer the risk because they can't afford to, and finds that it is also not feasible to accelerate, then the only option remaining is to just do nothing and hit the pothole at full speed. This is passive acceptance.

An example of active acceptance would be the driver having a spare tire ready prior to taking the trip and ensuring they have access to roadside assistance in case of any damage to the vehicle. These are examples of contingency plans to address the damage caused by the risk.

The secondary risk in this case is the same as the residual risk, which is also the same as the original risk that has been accepted.

Escalate: Escalation is almost always part of the communication plan and governance mandate, but it usually involves either "inform" or "support"—until the risk is deemed to be too much for the team to handle. In this case, the risk is most often escalated to the upper level to take charge. Typically, this means upper management is asked to take action, which may include making drastic changes in the team, removing or replacing members who were not effective in helping the project or the team in handling risks.

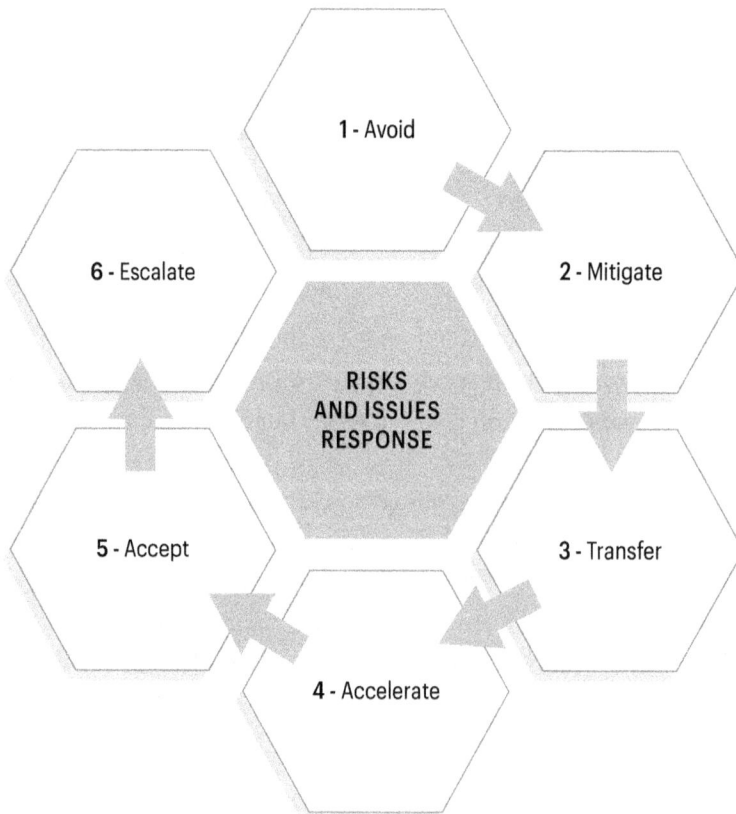

TYPES OF CRISES

There are many different types of crises, so it is difficult to be fully prepared for everything; however, it is helpful for a business to have a contingency outline in the event that plan assumptions prove inaccurate for any reason. This is particularly important because without a continency plan, a business may be slow to respond to catastrophic events and could face serious legal, operational, and reputational consequences.

A crisis management or contingency plan includes, for example:

- Operational communication plans—detailing the appropriate routes of communication to the proper internal and external audiences— ready to deploy quickly in the event of catastrophe.

- An operational backup power plan in the event that a catastrophe shuts down the power.

- A health and safety plan that can be used to address issues quickly, thereby enhancing safety measures for employees, customers, and suppliers.

- A plan for efficiently and quickly leaning down to skeleton operations if needed, or boosting operations to address immediate surges in certain practices, in order to ensure business continuity.

Contingency plans increase a company's reputation in the industry and instill confidence among customers and investors because the organization is thus seen as preemptive, ready to act, and fully prepared to address issues quickly.

The following are some useful steps in creating a meaningful crisis management or contingency plan:

- Identify crisis team members from different departments such as Operations, IT, Security, HR, Finance, and Legal. Suppliers may also be included. It is important to have a project management officer to enforce controls, ensure action tracking, direct communication channels, and make sure that team members are quickly completing the actions assigned to them.

- Identify possible types of crises, document the impact, and suggest resolutions for each type of crisis.

- Find out if any of the crises identified can be avoided. If not, see if it is possible for the company to handle them on their own or if efforts must be transferred to a third party.

- Figure out ways to protect the workforce, stabilize the supply chain, and continue to engage with customers.

- Identify critical functions and roles to keep the lights on and ensure continuity of business operations.

- Outline new policies and controls to limit access to systems and locations or authority to spend and hire during the crisis.

- Develop monitoring capabilities to continually examine crisis status and escalation while outlining possibilities of different scenarios and business impact.

- Document communication plans needed such as key emergency contacts, quick escalation procedures, toll-free numbers to call, media and social media handling, employee communication methods, and customer communication strategies.

- Complete financial stress-testing and develop triggers to be pulled depending on the magnitude of the impact.

- Do regular crisis-plan testing, training, maintaining, and updating.

A crisis that impacts businesses can be caused by an event happening internally or externally. The magnitude of the impact depends, of course, on the type and severity of such a crisis. The following are types of possible disasters to be included in the crisis management plan, as they can severely impact organizations.

Natural disasters: These are external factors and normally out of our control. Examples are pandemics, earthquakes, hurricanes, tornados, tsunamis, major storms, and floods. Although some of these come with no prior alarm, businesses can try to reduce their impact if they know they are in areas likely to be impacted. For example, hospitals can increase the amount of their personal protective equipment and sanitization and cleaning procedures to reduce virus spread, and buildings in areas likely to be hit by hurricanes or earthquakes can build structures that are resilient to such events.

Technological disasters: These can be internal or external factors. Examples include cyberattacks, data leaks, server shutdowns, and software crashes. Normally, if good measures are in place, such as using quality equipment, ensuring proper coding, employing dependable backup procedures, and having solid cybersecurity measures, then many of these technology-related crises can be avoided. However, if a technological crisis happens, the results can be devastating to business operations and an enterprise's reputation. The Equifax data breach was one of the worst ever on record, causing the personal information of more than 145 million people to be compromised. Not only did Equifax know of the system flaw the hackers took advantage of, but when the hack did happen, the firm waited a full two months before disclosing it.

Financial disasters: These can also be internal or external. Normally, financial disaster is internal, a result of bad business strategies that cause a decrease in customer demand, or colossal debt. Other times, financial disaster can be macro in nature and result from economic meltdown, such as the one that happened in 2008. In any of those cases, businesses experience a drop in value, depletion of cash, and inability to pay off obligations or offer acceptable solutions to customers. Usually, without extreme measures and government support such as stimulus packages and bailouts, businesses may not be able to overcome sudden and deep financial crises that hit them.

Personnel disasters: These crises are internal and often the result of illegal or unethical misconduct by an employee or someone associated with the company. Examples of this are insider trading, accepting bribes, discrimination, and sexual harassment. Many times, those behaviors result in significantly tarnishing an organization's reputation, especially if the perpetrator is a senior leader. A clear example is the Harvey Weinstein sexual assault cases that resulted in his company's collapse and filing for bankruptcy in 2018.

Organizational disasters: These are also always internal and can result in a business taking advantage of its customers rather than having a mutually beneficial relationship with them. Examples of these include Wells Fargo's 1.4 million fake accounts case and the company purposely charging 570,000 customers for insurances they did not need, Apple purposely slowing down older iPhones to force customers to upgrade, and United Airlines forcibly dragging a bloodied passenger off an overbooked flight.

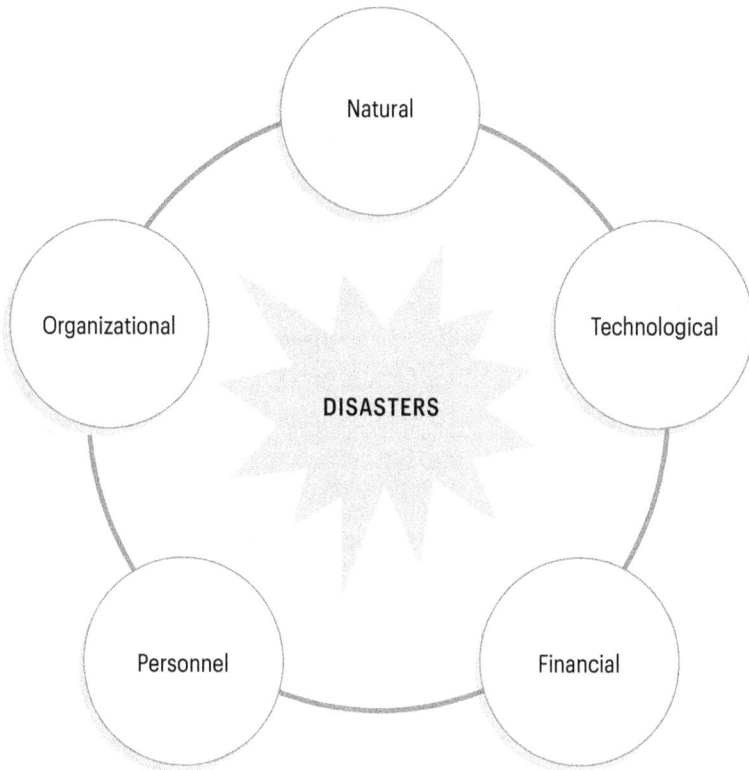

A DISASTER HAS HAPPENED: NOW WHAT?

Organizations can prepare to deal with catastrophic events by under-standing the stages in which they must react and determining how to respond to the events.

The following are sequential stages that companies go through when facing a crisis:

1. Warning: Most catastrophic events are unpredictable, but usually a crisis starts with signs looming on the horizon. Depending on the type of crisis, those warning signs can be in the form of a disease outbreak, a weather pattern, a financial KPI, a frequent pattern of complaints, or unusual customer or employee behavior. In this stage, companies should closely monitor the situation and escalate reports directly to senior management. Frequent updates as often as daily, and sometimes hourly, are necessary to evaluate the speed at which the events are occurring. The management team can also become proactive by blowing the dust off their contingency plans and having them ready, just in case.

2. Assessment: At this stage, companies should start to evaluate different scenarios to outline which direction a crisis can go; then, they can have their plans configured to address each scenario. The assessment should identify different escalation patterns and impacts and potential damages to the business, employees, customers, and community. Continuously monitoring risks and refreshing the contingency plans is the best course of action to take in order to quickly and effectively respond to the crisis at hand.

3. Responses: As the team may have created different possible scenarios and made their contingency plans ready in the previous stage, in this stage, it is about the speed and effectiveness with which management is able to activate certain triggers to address the outcomes of the developing crisis, depending on how the crisis evolves. Frequent communication is extremely critical at this stage. Daily, and many times hourly, standup calls or meetings are important in order to quickly react to any changes in the circumstances. War rooms can be assembled centrally and functionally to physically or virtually colocate key personnel who will handle the marching orders for activating necessary contingencies and to manage and mitigate the crisis.

4. Management: Depending on how the crisis situation evolves, managing the chosen plan becomes the most important stage in the process. Open communication with all stakeholders is vital. Most of the communication must come from the top senior executives in the form of personal, verbal, and written updates. It is recommended that a business have three main types of action: Painful, Distasteful, and Relatively Easy. It is probably best to start with the relatively easy actions to manage the situation. However, if those are not enough, then more serious action can be taken, and if these do not work, then some painful levers must be pulled. For example, one relatively easy maneuver would be to limit working hours to reduce cost in the case of a significant slowdown in demand. If that does not work, then some distasteful actions can be taken, such as closing some business outlets or operations. And if this does not prove effective, painful measures must be activated, such as a reduction in forces, cutting salaries, or even closure of the majority of the operating units, keeping only the most critical ones alive.

5. Resolutions: At this stage, the curve of events starts to flatten, and the crisis comes under control with good predictability of where the situation is heading. Usually, the sequence of events starts to normalize. Even though the crisis may still be in effect, certain business operations may start to slowly normalize, while others can start to get creative about how they can continue to offer solutions to their customers. Usually, people and companies are still suffering from the aftermath of the significant shock wave created by the catastrophic event. Ultimately, people and businesses begin to figure out ways to work around the situation. For example, in the spirit of adapting to change during the COVID-19 crisis in 2020, many businesses accepted the fact that they had to adhere to the "stay home" mandates and began working on creative ways to offer products and services to customers such as through home delivery, curbside pickup, distance learning, and video-based personal training workouts.

6. Recovery: At this stage, the crisis is over and the business can start to move quickly into recovery mode. Getting business back on track becomes a priority and employees begin resume their day-to-day lives, while customers tend to loosen up again and start placing orders or seeking services they were not able to enjoy during the crisis. It is interesting to observe that many businesses and individuals learn valuable lessons during catastrophic events. As a result, when they return to their normal operations, they are smarter and better than ever before. Some companies are unable to recover from the magnitude of damage encountered during a crisis, but those that can are usually set for a fresh, new start. Also, smart organizations usually spend some time at this stage analyzing the results of the catastrophe and how effective their crisis management plan was. They document lessons learned in order to avoid being in the same position during a similar situation in the future.

Conclusion

I wrote this book to provide a comprehensive perspective on how businesses can embrace change, develop an action-oriented mindset, adopt a customer-centric approach, leverage proven technology, enable a healthy culture to exploit market disruption, cope with catastrophic events, transform themselves, and deliver positive results.

As business leaders, professionals, or entrepreneurs, we should think less about what happened in the past and more about new opportunities. Disruptions will happen and perhaps even intensify over the next few decades. Therefore, the focus should be on what that means for our businesses. We need to know how to thrive, not only survive!

A maturity model may be a good idea for organizations to judge how well they are improving in elements such as profitability, culture, capabilities, processes, technology, tools, data, value creation, customer satisfaction, control, and governance. Certainly, some companies are more advanced in certain areas compared with others, but what matters is what their leaders are doing about it, and if they are putting in enough effort to move the critical elements higher in the maturity model.

Once our companies are accomplished in every one of those elements, our job is to ensure continued measures and improvement in the organizations, to ensure that they are always advancing toward optimization. This potentially enables them to operate and grow business exceptionally well and maintain a competitive advantage.

We should always strive to find the right balance between the legs of the three-legged stool: our strategies and tactics, delivery and project management, and efforts to build good culture, capabilities, and change management. If we lack any one of those elements, we miss the mark and deliver suboptimal results.

We should continually reevaluate our business models, evolve when we can, be nimble, and adapt our strategies and tactics in order to reach current and new goals. Continuous business improvement, optimization, and transformation are key to always satisfying our customers, shareholders, employees, and communities.

Endnotes

1 Mark J. Perry, "Only 52 US Companies Have Been on the Fortune 500 since 1955," AEI, blog, May 22, 2019, aei.org/ carpe-diem/only-52-us-companies-have-been-on-the-fortune-500-since-1955-thanks-to-the-creative-destruction-that-fuels-economic-prosperity/.

2 Leon C. Megginson, "Lessons from Europe for American Business," Southwestern Social Science Quarterly 44, no. 1 (1963): 4, jstor.org/stable/42866937.

3 See BrainyQuote, s.v. "Theodore Roosevelt Quotes," brainyquote.com/quotes/theodore_roosevelt_403358.

4 Clayton M. Christensen, Richard Alton, Curtis Rising, and Andrew Waldeck, "The Big Idea: The New M&A Playbook," Harvard Business Review, March 2011, hbr.org/2011/03/ the-big-idea-the-new-ma-playbook.

5 Gil Press, "6 Predictions about the Future of Digital Transformation," Forbes, December 6, 2015, forbes.com/ sites/gilpress/2015/12/06/6-predictions-about-the-future-of-digital-transformation/#178a6e921102.

6   Noel Randewich, "Tesla's Market Value Zooms Past That of GM and Ford—Combined," Reuters, January 8, 2020, reuters.com/article/us-usa-stocks-tesla/teslas-market-value-zooms-past-that-of-gm-and-ford-combined-idUSKBN1Z72M.

7   See BrainyQuote, s.v. "Oprah Winfrey Quotes," brainyquote.com/authors/oprah-winfrey-quotes.

8   Quoted in Jim Afremow, The Champion's Comeback: How Great Athletes Recover, Reflect, and Reignite (New York, NY: Rodale, 2016).

9   See Scrum Alliance, "The Agile Manifesto: The Key Values and Principles of Agile," scrumalliance.org/resources/agile-manifesto.

10 Goodreads, s.v. "W. Edwards Deming Quotes," goodreads.com/author/quotes/310261.W_Edwards_Deming.

11 Goodreads, s.v. "Herbert A. Simon Quotes," goodreads.com/author/quotes/89879.Herbert_A_Simon.

12 See BrainyQuote, s.v. "Wayne Gretzky Quotes," brainyquote.com/authors/wayne-gretzky-quotes.

13 See BrainyQuote, s.v. "Thomas Carlyle Quotes," brainyquote.com/authors/thomas-carlyle-quotes.

14 See BrainyQuote, s.v. "Albert Einstein Quotes," brainyquote.com/authors/albert-einstein-quotes.

15 You can find this information on Prosci's home page at prosci.com.

16 Please refer to prosci.com/adkar/adkar-model.

17 See Oxford Reference, s.v. "Alvin Toffler, 1928–2016, American Writer," oxfordreference.com/view/10.1093/acref/9780191826719.001.0001/q-oro-ed4-00010964.

18 Edgar Dale, Audio-Visual Methods in Teaching, 3rd ed. (New York, NY: Dryden Press, 1969).

19 See BrainyQuote, s.v. "Bill Gates Quotes," brainyquote.com/ authors/bill-gates-quotes.

20 Mind Tools Content Team, "Forming, Storming, Norming, and Performing: Understanding the Stages of Team Formation," Mind Tools, mindtools.com/pages/article/NewLDR_86.htm.

21 See Goodreads, s.v. "Richard Branson Quotes," goodreads .com/quotes/7356284-clients-do-not-come-first-employees- come-first-if-you.

About the Author

Rias Attar, also known as Giath Attar, is an accomplished business strategist, business transformation expert, operational excellence leader, and program and change management professional. He is an industry award winner executive with a track record of increasing profits and delivering strategic initiatives that have successfully transformed and integrated business operations. He is recognized for his ability to help strategize business architecture, identify areas in which to improve processes and outcomes, turn around businesses from deficiency to profitability, champion continuous improvement efforts, deliver challenging cross-functional programs while working collaboratively with diverse types of stakeholders, lead and coach winning teams, and inspire staff to welcome change and deliver ambitious results.

Mr. Attar has worked for various companies, from small to Fortune 500, and in a variety of industries in the United States, the Middle East, and Canada. He has a bachelor's degree in finance and a master's in business administration (MBA) from the University of Texas, and is certified as a Project Management Professional (PMP), Agile Certified Practitioner (ACP), Certified ScrumMaster (CSM), Lean Six Sigma Black Belt (LSSBB), and Change Management Practitioner (CMP).

Outside of work, Mr. Attar enjoys sports and music. He is a devoted family man and fortunate to have a beautiful wife (Sarab) and three lovely children (Sarah, Amir, and Yousef). His best time is with his kids—on the beach, playing board games, riding bikes, swimming, or just watching movies.

www.ingramcontent.com/pod-product-compliance
Lightning Source LLC
Chambersburg PA
CBHW051752200326
41597CB00025B/4533